**THE BRITISH
HORSE SOCIETY**

WESTMORLAND ON HORSEBACK

AVAILABLE IN THIS SERIES

The Cotswolds on Horseback
Wiltshire on Horseback
Westmorland on Horseback
The Ridgeway Downs on Horseback
Exmoor on Horseback
Somerset on Horseback
Hampshire on Horseback
Leicestershire on Horseback

First published 1994
by The British Horse Society
Access & Rights of Way Department
British Equestrian Centre
Stoneleigh Park, Kenilworth
Warwickshire CV8 2LR

A catalogue record for this book is available from the British Library

ISBN 1 899016 00 7

Printed by:
Tripod Press Limited, 7 Wise Street, Leamington Spa, CV31 3AP

Distribution: The British Horse Society, Stoneleigh Park, Kenilworth,
Warwickshire, CV8 2LR

Deer hunting

2

CONTENTS

ACKNOWLEDGEMENTS

The British Horse Society is grateful to the following people who have contributed to the preparation of this guide-book:

The trails were surveyed and described by Ann Aldridge, Elizabeth Craig, Helga Frankland, David and Helen Kerry, Katharine Pottinger, Nigel Redfern and Steve Sweeney.

The drawings are the work of Marilyn Leech and Betty Walker.

Alice Bondi, formerly of the East Cumbria Countryside Project, gave valuable editorial advice.

The map on page 44 is copied from Orlando Hodgson's map of Westmorland, published in 1828, by permission of the County Archivist, Cumbria County Council.

The book was compiled and edited by Nigel Redfern, British Horse Society County Bridleways Officer for Cumbria.

Forestry work using horse-power.

FOREWORD

The '.................. on Horseback' series of published rides launched in 1993 has proved extremely popular. This confirms the British Horse Society's belief that many riders need information on routes known to be open, available and providing pleasurable riding.

Many volunteers have worked to research these routes, thus helping to contribute to the Countryside Commission's target of having all rights of way defined, open and signed by the year 2000. This Society wholeheartedly supports this aim which it incorporates into its Access & Rights of Way strategy for the last decade of this Century.

Together with our booklet 'Bed & Breakfast for Horses', these publications enable riders and carriage drivers to plan holidays and other trips. This extends the pleasure and value of owning a horse either to ride or drive, and enables an assortment of different experiences to be enjoyed be they landscape, flora and fauna or historic sites and buildings.

Equestrianism provides one of the most intense pleasures of life, wholly understood only by those who ride, or drive carriages. The Society is proud to contribute in some way to the fulfilment of that pleasure. The challenges of research and development of further routes will continue to be explored.

E A T BONNOR-MAURICE
Chairman, British Horse Society

March 1994

The British Horse Society's ARROW Project aims to identify open and usable routes of varying length and shape (circular, figure-of-eight or linear) to help riders and carriage drivers to enjoy the countryside by means, as far as possible, of the network of public rights of way and the minor vehicular highways. This collection of rides is the result of research and mapping by volunteers who took up the challenge of the ARROW initiative with such enthusiasm and effort.

I am faced with the equally daunting challenge of writing an introductory chapter. Should I write reams about each topic or try simply to point you in the right direction? I have decided upon the second method as the search for information is itself highly educative and stays in the mind better than reading it all in one place. Also, since we all have different expectations of our holiday, a very full guide seemed wrong. Nevertheless, there are a few pointers I would like to suggest to you.

The most important one is to start your planning several months in advance of the trip, including a visit to the area you intend to ride in. You should make endless lists of things to DO (e.g. get the saddle checked) and things to CHECK OUT (can you read a map, for instance). You may find joining the local BHS Endurance Riding Group very helpful, as there you will meet people who can give you information about the degree of fitness needed for yourself and your horse (feeding for fitness not dottiness) , and many other useful hints on adventurous riding. You may also enjoy some of the Pleasure rides organised by the group or by the local Riding Club. These are usually about 15-20 miles and you ride in company, though using a map. You may find them under the title Training Rides. These rides will get both of you used to going into strange country. If you usually ride on well-known tracks, then your horse will find it nerve-racking to go off into new territory, and you yourself may also find the excitement of deep country a bit surprising, so try to widen your experience at home before you go off on holiday.

ACCOMMODATION

Decide how far you wish to ride each day of your holiday, book overnight accommodation for both of you and if possible visit it to see if the five-star suite on offer to your horse is what he is used to. Decide if you want to stable him or to turn him out at the end of the day, and arrange to drop off some food for him, as he will not relish hard work on a diet of green grass, nor will he enjoy a change in his usual food. If you are to have a back-up vehicle, of course, then you will not need to do some of this, but you should certainly make a preliminary visit if you can. The BHS publish a Bed & Breakfast Guide for Horses which is a list of people willing to accommodate horses, and sometimes riders, overnight. The Society does not inspect these places, so you should check everything in advance.

FITNESS

You and your horse should be fit. For both of you , this is a process taking about two months. If you and/or your horse are not in the full flush of youth, then it may take a bit longer. The office chair, the factory floor, or the household duties do not make or keep you fit, but carefully planned exercise will. Remember that no matter how fit your horse seems, he does not keep himself fit - you get him fit. There are several books with details of fitness programmes for a series of rides. Do not forget to build in a rest day during your holiday - neither of you can keep going all the time, day after day. Miles of walking may get you fit, but it uses different muscles from riding; you may get a surprise when you start riding longer distances. It seems to me that the further you intend to ride, the longer your preparation should be. Nothing can be done in a hurry.

Your horse should be obedient, so work on that. If you want him to stand, then he must stand. If you want to go through water, then he must be prepared to walk down a slope or even step down off a bank to go through the stream, so start with puddles and insist that he go through the middle. Does he help you open gates? I hope so, or you will have a great deal of mounting and dismounting to do. Does he tie up - this is essential if you are to have a peaceful pint at lunchtime.

MAPS

Can you read a map? Can you make and read a grid reference (usually referred to as GR)? Get a Pathfinder map of your area and take yourself for a walk and see if you end up where you expect to. Learn to know exactly where you are on the map, and how to understand the symbols (if your map shows hilly ground, the journey will take longer). Can you work out how long a ride is in miles and roughly how long it will take? You will be using rights of way and it is very important that you stay in the line of the path - that is the only place you have a right to be, and you may deviate from that line only as much as is necessary to get you round an obstruction on the path. You are going to be riding over land that forms part of someone's work place and that fact must be respected. It is only by the efforts of farmers and landowners that the countryside exists in its present form - so that we may enjoy it as we pass by.

You will need to know the grid reference (GR.) of the start and end of the various tracks you are to use. Get a copy of an Ordnance Survey (OS) Landranger map and really learn the details on the right-hand side, some of which explain how to arrive at a Grid Reference. Learn to go in the door (Eastings - from left to right) and up the stairs (Northings - from bottom to top). There is a great deal of information on the Landranger maps and not so much on the Pathfinders, but the Pathfinder gives more details on the map itself, so that is the map you will use for the actual ride. Or you may care to buy a Landranger of the area you are visiting and, using a highlighter pen, mark in all the rides you want to make, so that you can see through the marks you make. Then get from any Outdoor shop a map case which will allow you to read the map without taking it out of the case and which you can secure round yourself. Also, you should know if you are facing north, south, east or west as you ride. Quite important if you think about it, as it is no good riding into the sunset if you are meant to be going south. Plastic orienteering compasses are cheap and reliable.

TACK

Have your tack thoroughly checked by your saddler, as there is nothing so annoying as a sore back which could have been prevented, or an unnecessarily broken girth strap. How are you going to carry the essential headcollar and rope each day? What about spare shoes, or a false shoe?

What to take on the ride depends on how

much back-up you have. If you have to carry a change of clothes, etc., then you are into very careful planning indeed - balance saddle bag, the lot. If you are based at your first night stop all the time, then life is much easier. You should always carry a first aid kit for horse and rider. You will also have to plan how to wash the girth and numnah. Remember our delightful climate and always carry a waterproof and additional warm clothing - it never pays to gamble with rain and wind.

SAFETY

It is always wiser to ride in company. The other person can always hold your horse, or pull you out of the ditch, as well as being someone to talk to about the excitements of the day and to help plan everything. You should always wear a BSI riding hat, properly secured, and also safe footwear. You need a clearly defined heel and a smooth sole. Even if riding in company, tell someone where you are going and roughly how long you expect to take. If affordable, take a portable telephone. Make a list of the things you must carry every day and check it before leaving base.

INSURANCE

You should have Third Party Legal Liability Insurance. This will protect you if you or your horse cause a bit of mayhem (accidentally!). Membership of the BHS gives you this type of insurance, plus Personal Accident Insurance as part of the membership package. Check your household insurance to make sure it covers riding before you rely only on that, as some insurances do not. You should always have this type of cover when venturing forth into the outside world, even if it is an hour's hack from home.

PARKING

If you intend to box to the start of the day's ride, either have someone to take the box away or make sure it is safely, securely and considerately parked. If you have to make arrangements to park, do it well in advance or the contact may well have gone to market or the hairdressers when you make a last minute call. Have the vehicle number etched on to the windows for security.

MONEY

This is vital, so work out a system of getting money if necessary. Sadly we can no longer gallop up to the bank and lead Dobbin into the cashier's queue, nor do most banks have hitching rails. Post Offices are more numerous and might be a useful alternative. Always have the price of a telephone call on you.

Lastly, if you do run into problems of blocked paths or boggy ones, write to the Highway Authority of the relevant county council and tell them. Then you can do something about it. You might even think of adopting a path near home and keeping an eye on it, telling your own county council of any difficulties you encounter. It is through such voluntary work that these rides have been made possible.

Wherever you ride, always do it responsibly, with care of the land, consideration for the farmer and courtesy for all other users. Remember the Country Code and enjoy your ARROW Riding.

I hope this chapter will have started you planning and making lists. If I seem to be always writing about forward planning it is only because I usually leave things to the last minute, which causes chaos!

PHILIPPA LUARD

WESTMORLAND
by Jennifer MacKenzie

The lakes and mountains of the old county of Westmorland form one of the most breath-taking and beautiful landscapes in England.

Rugged peaks, some rising to more than 3000 ft, are mirrored in tranquil lakes, a scenery which has inspired countless poets, writers and artists; however, in days gone by this picturesque but rough terrain often proved difficult for transport and communications.

People depended on horses. Sure-footed ponies picked their way over high mountain passes to deliver goods, and sometimes carried smugglers' hoards or even corpses for burial, for miles over the shortest routes to their destination.

It is only within the last 200 years that the 'transport revolution' has opened up Cumbria to outside influences. The improvements in communication were late in coming and even by the middle of the 18th century there were few wheeled vehicles in the region and people either walked or travelled on horseback, the women usually seated on pillions behind the men.

Today, one of the best ways to enjoy Westmorland is on horseback. Many of these ancient tracks and byways trodden by previous generations of Cumbrians and their working ponies can now be enjoyed by riders for pleasure.

The Romans built the first roads to serve their military needs. Many of these routes first charted nearly 2000 years ago are used by motor traffic today, but some form the bridleways which cross the fells.

High Street is certainly the best known of all the Roman roads in the Lake District. The route along the high fells of eastern Lakeland has given its name to the highest of those hills, at 2718 ft above sea level.

The trading system of medieval times went hand in hand with the growth of a network of paths and tracks along which produce was moved. This unplanned growth was in contrast to that of the Romans: very few roads are known to have been built in the Middle Ages - new routes just came into being when they were used often enough.

During the 13th century trade was beginning to flourish in Cumbria. The growth of the cloth industry based on local supplies of wool enabled Kendal to become the collecting centre for woollen cloth made throughout the area. Mining and quarrying were also becoming increasingly important.

The population of remote areas was very sparse, so that medieval parishes were very large and the dead often had to be carried a great distance to their parish church for burial. Some routes were used for hardly any other purpose and became known locally as a 'corpse road'. Some of these are still named as such on modern Ordnance Survey maps even though their use as corpse roads ended several hundred years ago.

By the 17th century cattle were carving wide roads across the countryside as Cumbrian farms were actively engaged in the trade. Scottish cattle were bought in the autumn and fattened for sale in the spring. The drove roads, some of which survive, were the route for the cattle to the south - a trade which was running at the rate of 80,000 head a year by the early 19th century.

Before 1750 it was practically impossible to drive wheeled vehicles westward from Kendal so before the construction of turnpike roads most goods had to be moved by packhorse.

Kendal, the centre of the woollen trade, was served by a number of packhorse routes. More than twenty gangs of packhorses worked from the town each week, travelling both within the county and as far afield as Hull, Wigan and Glasgow. While the packhorse was reliable, it was slow, the journey to London for example taking more than two weeks. Moving in a single file, a train would consist of up to thirty horses each carrying a 3 cwt load. These packhorse trains remained a feature of Cumbrian rural life until the middle of the 19th century when the new railways took the trade over.

Until then the Fell pony, which has roamed the northern hills for centuries, was used as a packhorse. They were well fitted to the job, being strong, sure-footed and fast walkers. This versatile breed was used as draught animals both on farms and in towns and villages.

Fell ponies have been registered in stud books since 1898 and the breed has survived both economic and social pressures to remain today as one of the purest of the British breeds. Some herds can still be seen on the fells where they breed in a semi-wild state. Earlier this century the breed was under threat as the use of horse power diminished, but vital financial help came from King George V and from Mrs Heelis, better known as the author Beatrix Potter, who had a great affection for the breed.

The breed is immortalised in the Fell Pony Museum at Dalemain, a historic house near Ullswater which dates back to Elizabethan times and has a fine Georgian facade. Both the house and its gardens are open to the public. The Fell Pony Society holds its annual stallion and colt show at Dalemain in early May and its breed show at Brougham, near Penrith, in mid-August.

One of the county's more recent events is the Lowther Horse Driving Trials - renamed the Lowther Event in 1993 to mark its 21st anniversary. The three-day event held in Lord Lonsdale's Lowther Park, south of Penrith, in early August has become an institution enjoyed both by local people and by thousands of visitors. It began purely as horse driving trials and attracts top class competition including Prince Philip and former world champion George Bowman, from Penrith. There are classes of every sort for horse and pony enthusiasts and the country fair has a wide range of exhibitions portraying all aspects of country life.

A more traditional gathering, although equally famous, is the Appleby Horse Fair, held during the week after the Derby. Appleby-in-Westmorland is completely taken over for six days in early June by the huge gypsy gathering, the largest of its kind in the world. The horse fair has survived under the protection of a charter since 1685 and it is still all about horse trading. Those who don't intend to buy or sell come for a good time and a 'crack'. The event is a spectacle with every type of horse on parade from trotters to Clydesdales to magnificent stallions ridden bareback.

William Wordsworth's vision for the future foresaw the creation of the Lake District National Park 'in which every man has a right and interest who has an eye to perceive and a heart to enjoy'. It was Wordsworth who called the Lake District 'the loveliest spot that man hath ever found' - and few who have been here would disagree.

RIDING IN WESTMORLAND

This book describes a network of 16 riding routes in the area bounded by the main roads between Penrith, Appleby, Kirkby Stephen, Tebay, Kendal and Windermere, an area which includes most of the old county of Westmorland. These trails vary in length from 8 to 29 miles (13 to 47 km): they provide a total of about 210 miles (337 km) of riding, of which 153 miles (246 km) are on bridleways, byways or unmetalled roads; 15 miles (24 km) on unfenced motor roads; and 42 miles (67 km) on other roads, some of which have wide verges.

Heavy traffic is not generally a problem, but there are just a few places, on very narrow roads with no verges, where even one vehicle may make things difficult. The A6 road bisects the area, and several of these trails cross it. It is a single carriageway, usually without much traffic, but you still have to take care in crossing.

GRADING
The trails are graded according to their severity, as follows:

Grade 1: easy going, with no problems likely.

Grade 2: including some moderately severe conditions, usually of steep gradients, rocky broken surfaces, soft going, featureless landscape, or the risk of mist at high level; but within the scope of any competent rider who can read a map.

Grade 3: including conditions which many riders may find severe and which some may feel to be unsuitable for them or for their horses: similar conditions to Grade 2 but more so.

THE MAPS
There is a map for each of the trails described, indicating how apparent it is on the ground:

'obvious': usually either a metalled road or an enclosed track.

'indistinct': the line of the route can be seen on the ground because it has some definite feature; but is not obvious and could be missed.

'invisible': the line of the route cannot usually be seen.

These maps are not a substitute for the 1:25,000 Ordnance Survey maps, which are essential.

SAFETY
On average about 20 people die on the Lake District hills each year. Few of them are rock climbers who fall: many are walkers who are simply not properly prepared

and equipped. Always observe the following rules whenever you ride on the hills, in order to reduce the risk of mishap or worse:

1. Ensure that your route, destination and expected time of arrival are known, so that you would be missed if you did not arrive and rescuers would know where to search. The Mountain Rescue Service - manned by volunteers - can be called by dialling 999.

2. Always carry with you the appropriate 1:25,000 Ordnance Survey map, and a compass. These maps are the Pathfinder series, in green covers, or in the case of the Lake District the Outdoor Leisure Series.

3. Note the weather forecast, and do not go if it is unfavourable. The local forecast can be obtained by telephoning 0891 500719.

4. Not all horses are suitable for some of the routes in this network: think about whether yours is likely to be happy on steep slopes and rocky surfaces, or on boggy ground. Native ponies are much more likely to be sensible about bogs than most other horses.

5. Always ride with a headcollar and lead rope as well as a bridle, or with a combined headcollar bridle, so that you can tie up when you stop.

6. Take with you more warm clothing than you think you will need, and a survival bag.

7. Remember that if your horse should become disabled you may have to walk for a long distance over rough country: footwear should be suitable for walking as well as riding.

8. Take some emergency rations.

9. Never ride alone: you would be alone when you needed help.

10. If you have to leave an injured person alone while you seek help, make sure that you know where to come back to - not as easy as it may seem when you are leaving.

Most of these routes go through industrial areas: the industry is agriculture. Although you have a right of way, it is always better to think of that right as a privilege; and occasionally it may be tactful not to cause inconvenience to a farmer by pressing on regardless.

Some bridleways, particularly on heavy land, deteriorate rapidly in wet weather and should be avoided during and soon after heavy rain.

Always ride in a careful and responsible manner, remembering the needs of other users. Walkers, for example, may easily be alarmed by the sudden appearance of horses, particularly on a narrow path. Equally, horses are often alarmed by the sudden appearance of mountain bikes.

Follow the advice of the Country Code:
>Enjoy the countryside and respect its life and work.
>Guard against all risk of fire
>Fasten all gates
>Keep your dogs under close control
>Keep to the bridleways across farmland
>Avoid damaging fences, hedges and walls
>Leave livestock, crops and machinery alone
>Take your litter home
>Help to keep all water clean
>Protect wildlife, plants and trees
>Take special care on country roads
>Make no unnecessary noise

We do hope you will enjoy riding in Westmorland.

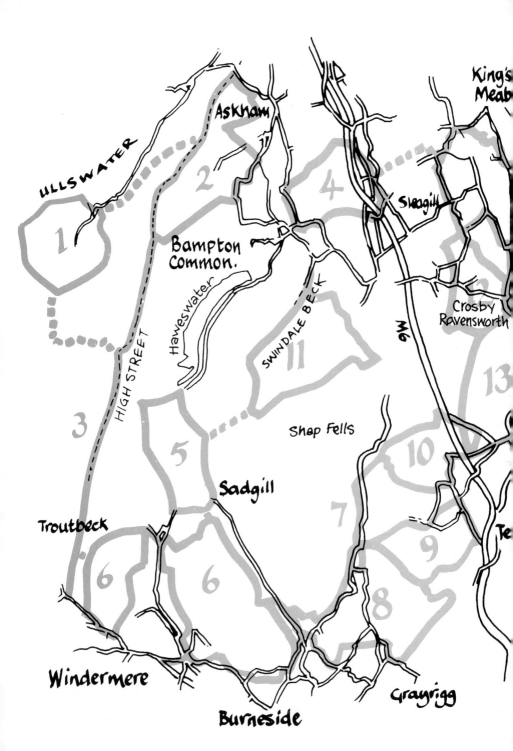

ULLSWATER

Askham

King's Meab

1

2

4

Sleagill

Bampton Common.

Haweswater

HIGH STREET

SWINDALE BECK

Crosby Ravensworth

M6

11

13

3

Shap Fells

5

10

Sadgill

Troutbeck

7

6

6

9

Te

8

Windermere

Grayrigg

Burneside

14

WESTMORLAND
ON HORSEBACK

━━━━━━━━━━ The route of the trails described.

▪ ▪ ▪ ▪ ▪ Link routes referred to in the text,
but not described.

Links which are only motor roads are not shown.

KEY

═══ ─ ─ ─   **ROADS**

+ + + + + + +   **BYWAYS**

_ _ _ _ _ _   **BRIDLEWAYS**

THE BLUE OVERPRINTED ROUTE-LINE AS BELOW ALSO
INDICATES THE VISIBILITY "ON THE GROUND" OF THE
ROUTE TO THE USER.

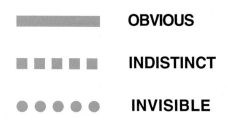

▬▬▬▬▬   **OBVIOUS**

■ ■ ■ ■ ■   **INDISTINCT**

● ● ● ● ●   **INVISIBLE**

The distances in boxes are cumulative from the start.

PATTERDALE TO MARTINDALE

TRAIL 1

AN 8 MILE (13 KM) CIRCULAR TRAIL (CLOCKWISE)

Ordnance Survey Map: The English Lakes NE Sheet (1:25,000)

Route: Patterdale - Silver Crag - Sandwick - Martindale - Beda Fell - Boredale Hause

Parking & Starting Point: Parking may be possible at Side Farm (GR.398163) if they are not too busy; otherwise at the car park in Patterdale. There is road access to the northern side of this trail, but it would entail driving a horsebox up Martindale Hause, which is very steep and has numerous hairpin bends. It is possible, but not recommended.

Trail Grade: 2. Parts of this trail are very rocky, and careful riding is essential. There is no access to emergency vehicles between Blowick (GR.396174) and Scalehow (GR.415192), or between Beda Fell (GR.425162) and Rooking Gill (GR.402161).

Of Interest:
The views are spectacular throughout this ride: firstly along the side of Ullswater; then Martindale is charming; then the climb up Beda Fell, with the wilderness of Bannerdale on your left, and finally the sight of Helvellyn and many other majestic peaks as you descend from Boredale Hause.

Martindale is a haunt of Red Deer, which are Britain's largest land mammal. They have keen senses, particularly of scent and hearing, and live in the woods and on the open hill in several parts of the coun-

try. The sexes tend to live apart for most of the year, although 'knobbers' - young males under 16 months - may be found with hinds until the rut, usually in mid-October. The calves are born in early June; if found they should be left to await their mother's return. They are weaned between late October and January. In April the stags cast their antlers which begin re-growing immediately, and they are usually 'clean' or in hard horn by mid-August.

The Martindale herd is particularly special because they are descended from the only indigenous English Red Deer after the last Ice Age, having avoided the hybridisation to which some English herds were subject. Red Deer are stalked for sport and to maintain herd size and health between 1st August and the end of February.

Boredale Hause, (GR.408158), is 1309 ft. (399 m) above sea level. William Wordsworth, who came this way in November 1805, described the scene vividly: 'Our ascent even to the top was very easy; when it was accomplished we had exceedingly fine views, some of the lofty Fells being resplendent with sunshine, and others partly shrouded by clouds. Ullswater, bordered by black steeps, was of dazzling brightness; the plain beyond Penrith smooth and bright, or rather gleamy, as the sea or sea sands'. There was formerly a small chapel on Boredale Hause which even in Wordsworth's day was a ruin. He was impressed by its exposed situation: 'One cannot pass by

17

without being reminded that the rustic psalmody must have had the accompaniment of many a wildly-whistling blast; and what dismal storms must often have drowned the voice of the preacher!'.

Route Description:

From Side Farm turn left north-westwards along an unmetalled road, past the camp site on your left. *The fell on the right with the rocky slopes is Place Fell (2155ft, 657m).* Keep to the main track, following the wall, where another track goes off to the right. Continue along a stony track, around Silver Crag, with wonderful views of the lake. *(Birk Fell is on the right).* You go along the lake side, through the woods. *The bridleway is very steep and rough in places; steps have been put in to stop erosion, which makes hard going for horses.* At Scalehow (GR.416192), ford the beck - *the horses can get a drink here.* Ride on along the track - the going is rather easier now - to Sandwich (GR.423196) (3.5 miles: 5.7 km). *Ahead, Hallin Fell (1273 feet, 388 m) is a prominent landmark.*

Turn right along the road, which is unfenced, and take the next turn left, at Doe Green (GR.426192). Cross the bridge over the Boredale Beck and go through the gate ahead. Bear right, then through the gate on the left on to a grassy track. Climb uphill to a wicket gate at the top - *beware of barking dogs!* - and on up to the road. Turn left, and after about 200 yards (180 m) take a well-defined track on the right (GR.432191). *(The bridleway from Barton Fell (Trail 3) past Howtown joins the road you have just left, about a quarter of a mile (400 m) further on).*

The track, between stone walls, joins the road again at Winter Crag (GR.433183) (4.6 miles: 7.4 km). Here the route turns right, but a short diversion in the opposite direction would bring you to Martindale Old Church, built in 1633, which is well worth a visit. From Winter Crag, follow the road south for just over a mile (1.9 km) to Dale Head (GR.434165) (5.8 miles: 9.4 km). The road is narrow, mainly between walls though unfenced in places, but there is very little traffic. *Beda Head (1670ft : 509 m) marks the highest point of the ridge on your right.*

Don't go into the farmyard at Dale Head but through the wicket on your right. Follow the track over a little stream, past the farm on to a good track. Where the track divides, bear right to go diagonally up the side of Beda Fell - signed to Patterdale. Go through the next gate on to the open fell. *The track is mainly grassy, with one or two rocky places but not too difficult.*

Boredale Hause, (GR.408158), is 1309 ft. (399 m) above sea level. When you reach the top, (7.6 miles: 12.3 km) the path turns right to a cairn, then left along the other side of the ridge.

The bridleway from Hartsop meets your route here. The path gradually descends, fairly narrow but well-defined - mostly grassy. You cross a little stream - *another chance to water the horses* - with a rocky scramble up the other side. *There are some wet places on Boredale Hause, so take care to pick your way.*

The track from the Hause to Side Farm is steep and stony, and great care is

18

needed. It divides into two, the upper one being the bridleway, but they are equally rough! However the path soon levels out and, just past a stand of larch trees, there is a steep track on your left down to a gate; go through that and immediately through another on your right. Ride along the road for a short way to arrive back at Side Farm.

TRAIL 1.

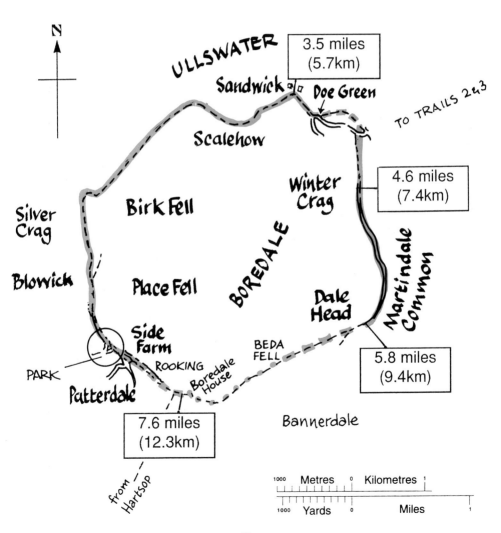

SAFETY

Know your Highway Code
(1994 Edition)

*In Particular
Paragraphs 216/224*

The Country Code should be observed by every rider, with great care being taken to keep to the line of the Public Rights of Way particularly when crossing farmland.

ASKHAM TO LOADPOT HILL

TRAIL 2

A 14 MILE (23 KM) CIRCULAR TRAIL (ANTI-CLOCKWISE)

Ordnance Survey Map: The English Lakes NE Sheet (1:25,000)

Route: Askham - Winder Hall - Barton Fell - Loadpot Hill - Cockle Hill - Heltondale -Ketley Gate - Riggingleys Top

Parking & Starting Point: Take the road to the west in Askham village, go up the hill and across the cattle grid, and park beside the road, at GR.506235. This is where your ride begins.

Trail Grade: 2. The going is generally good on this ride, but mist may be a hazard. In the event of an emergency it would not be accessible to a four-wheel drive vehicle south of Elder Beck (GR.482222).

Of Interest:

In the area of Cawdale - 7.3 miles: 11.8 km into your ride - there are usually several herds of Fell ponies to be seen. The Fell pony, one of our native breeds, is a sturdy animal of distinctive appearance. Colours may be black, brown, bay or grey with little or no white marking. The height limit is 14hh, but most do not exceed 13.3 hh.

Hardy enough to breed and winter on the hills, these strong, hard-working ponies were for centuries the only form of transport in the Lake District. Lines of them often 'loose-headed', could be seen carrying woolpacks to Kendal; ore from the mines and slate from the quarries, along the packways and drove roads of Cumbria. In the west these intelligent and sure-footed

ponies conspired with smugglers to haul brandy, tobacco and other contraband goods away through the night over the hills from their landing places on the coast. They are still just as versatile. A good ride for a competent adult, they will also look after a child or carry a tourist trekking; or turn their hooves to hunting, jumping, or driving where their good trotting pace comes into its own.

Route Description:

Go through the gate opposite your parking spot and up the bridleway to the north-west between stone walls. Turn right at the T-junction. *There is a fine view half-right of the ruins of Lowther Castle, built by Robert Smirke in the Gothic style for the Earl of Lonsdale in 1806.* Turn left when you reach the minor road. A mile (1.6 km) further on, turn left on to a bridleway to Winder Hall Farm, signed High Street. At the farm (1.9 miles: 3.1 km), bear right and continue on the track up the hill and through a gate out on to the fell. Turn left, and ride up the hill with the wood on your left.

This leads to another bridleway, a good track which you join at GR.490240 and turn right. Ride on round the shoulder of Heughscar Hill where there is a glorious view of Ullswater and the fells beyond. At the bridleway crossing (GR.483227), ride straight across. For the next two miles there are some boggy places but the route is passable with care.

Just before you come to the Elder Beck you will find The Cockpit a few yards to the left. This is an embanked stone circle 85 feet (26 m) in diameter, thought to date from the Early Bronze Age about 4000 years ago.

Cross the beck by the ford (GR.482222) (3.6 miles: 5.8 km) and keep going on the main track. Cross the Aik Beck by another ford and bear left on to a grass track through the bracken. *As you ride up towards Arthur's Pike there is a panoramic view extending from Saddleback in the west, to Carrock Fell overlooking the plain, the Scottish hills in the distance, and the Pennine range to the east.*

For part of the way behind Arthur's Pike the track is marked by cairns, but don't be misled by two cairns on the right which mark a different track. At GR.461198 you rejoin the line of High Street, *the road which the Romans built to connect their fort at Ambleside with that at Brougham, near Penrith. The route along this bleak and often snowbound ridge seems a strange situation for a major road; but it was probably more accessible than the lower ground which was rocky and heavily wooded. Traces of the Roman construction are still to be found.*

The track continues up towards Loadpot Hill, then southwards along the contour, which is at 2000 ft (610 m). *As you bear left to ride uphill again there are more dramatic views of the Lakeland hills to the south-west.* At the top of the slope the track leads round, just south of the hill top, across a concrete slab which is the site of Lowther House, formerly a shooting lodge with stables (7.3 miles: 11.8 km).

The High Street bridleway (Trail 3) continues southwards, but you bear left and ride on down the slope with Cawdale 1000 feet (300 m) below on your right.

As you ride north-eastwards the going is good, but the route is not easily seen all the way: ahead of you, two miles (3.2 km) from Loadpot Hill, there is a small belt of woodland. Aim for the left-hand end of this shelter belt, and turn left at the minor road a quarter of a mile (0.4 km) further on (9.9 miles: 16.0 km).

This is an unenclosed road which leads down to Heltondale one and a quarter miles (2.0 km) away and goes on to join the road between Helton and Bampton, (GR.507211) (11.4 miles: 18.4 km). Here you turn left immediately, up a road signed Widewath Farm. Where the road turns left to the farm, ride straight on up the bridleway, a track between stone walls. Go through a gate out on to the fell, then ahead for about 50 yards (45 m) and bear right up a grass track through the bracken. You cross a minor road and the bridleway continues, signed Howtown and Pooley Bridge.

A mile further on, at the bridleway crossing at Ketley Gate (13.0 miles: 20.9 km), turn right towards Askham. You go up the hill to Riggingleys Top, through a gate in the wall, and down again to return to your starting place.

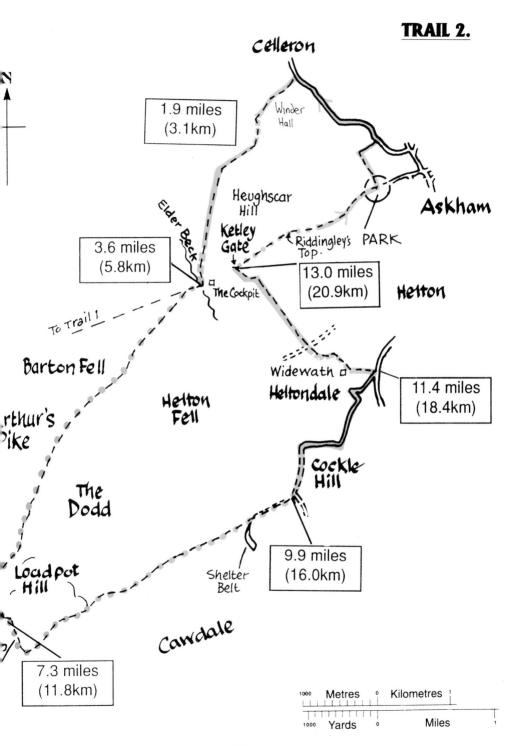

TRAIL 2.

Celleron

N

Winder Hall

1.9 miles
(3.1km)

Heughscar Hill

Ketley Gate

Elder Beck

Askham

Riddingley's Top.

PARK

3.6 miles
(5.8km)

The Cockpit

13.0 miles
(20.9km)

Helton

To Trail 1

Barton Fell

Widewath

Heltondale

11.4 miles
(18.4km)

rthur's Pike

Helton Fell

The Dodd

Cockle Hill

Loadpot Hill

Shelter Belt

9.9 miles
(16.0km)

Cawdale

7.3 miles
(11.8km)

1000 Metres 0 Kilometres 1

1000 Yards 0 Miles 1

23

EXPLORE
LAKELAND
THE EASY WAY

Escorted trail rides on our horses or yours. Rides available from one hour to a few days. Accommodation for horse and rider and all transfers arranged.

05394 43811

WYNLASS BECK STABLES
Windermere, Cumbria
LA23 1EU
BHS and ABRS Approved

Disclaimer

Whilst all due care was taken in the preparation of these maps neither the British Horse Society nor their agents or servants accept any responsibility for any inaccuracies which may occur. It should be borne in mind that landmarks and conditions change and it is assumed that the user has a Pathfinder Ordnance Survey map and a compass.

TRAIL 3

A 17 MILE (27 KM) DIRECT TRAIL (SOUTHWARDS)

Ordnance Survey Maps: The English Lakes NE & SE Sheets (1:25,000)

Route: Winder Hall Farm - Barton Fell - Arthur's Pike - Loadpot Hill - High Raise - High Street - Park Fell - Lowther Brow - Longmire Road

Parking & Starting Point: Parking may be available by prior arrangement with Mr Carruthers at Winder Hall Farm (GR.492246), telephone (07684) 86372. The starting point of the ride is the bridleway at Winder Hall Farm. There is no long-stay parking place at the southern end of High Street, but there is room to load.

Trail Grade: 3. This ride includes some steep gradients, rocky surfaces, and in one or two places a narrow track with a long way to fall. Much of the distance is at a height of more than 2000 feet (600m) above sea level and mist is a frequent hazard. In the event of emergency there would be no access for vehicles between Elder Beck (GR.482222) and Hagg Gill (GR.428080). There may be no opportunity to water the horses for ten miles (16km) after crossing Aik Beck (GR.473220).

Of Interest:
For much of the way this trail follow s the course of High Street, the road which the Romans built to connect their fort at Ambleside with that at Brougham, near Penrith. The route along this bleak and often snowbound ridge seems a strange situation for a major road; but it was probably more accessible than the lower

ground which was rocky and heavily wooded. Traces of the Roman construction are still to be found. The plateau on the top of High Street is known as Racecourse Hill: there were formerly race meetings held here, probably for Fell ponies; and it was also the site of a shepherds' meet, to which stray sheep were taken, and claimed by their owners.

Route Description:

The trail starts at the bridleway to Winder Hall Farm, (signed High Street). At the farm, bear right and continue on the track up the hill and through a gate out on to the fell. Turn left, and ride up the hill keeping the wood on your left. This leads to another bridleway (GR.490240), a good track, where you turn right. Ride along this track and round the shoulder of Heughscar Hill where there is a glorious view of Ullswater and the fells beyond. At the bridleway crossing (GR.483227), ride straight across. *For the next two miles there are some boggy places but the route is passable with care.*

Just before you come to Elder Beck, you will find The Cockpit a few yards to the left. This is an embanked stone circle 85 feet (26 m) in diameter, thought to date from the Early Bronze Age about 4000 years ago.

After 2.1 miles (3.4 km) cross the beck by the ford (GR.482222) and keep going along the main track. Cross Aik Beck by another ford and bear left on to a

grass track through the bracken. *As you ride up towards Arthur's Pike there is a panoramic view extending from Saddleback in the West, to Carrock Fell overlooking the plain, the Scottish hills in the distance, and the Pennine range to the east.* For part of the way behind Arthur's Pike the track is marked by cairns, but don't be misled by two cairns on the right which mark a different track. Rejoin the line of High Street at GR.461198.

Continue along the track up towards Loadpot Hill, then south-westwards along the contour. *As you bear left to ride uphill again there are more dramatic views of the Lakeland hills to the south-west. At the foot of the slope you are at the 2000 feet (610 m) contour.*

Continue to ride southwards, ignoring the bridleway down to Cawdale (see Trail 2), which swings round to the east (5.8 miles: 9.3 km). *From here to Thornthwaite Crag the going is generally good turf, but you always have to look out for boggy areas which can be treacherous.* Ride down the southern slope of Loadpot Hill and up again for one mile to Wether Hill. Ride up the eastern shoulder of Red Crag and from then on the ridge becomes

narrower. You will meet a wall that swings up the hill from the right and you follow it for about 300 yards (275 m) before crossing to the other side. Ride on for one mile with the wall on your left and go through a gate on the slope of High Raise (GR.449138). The bridleway across the top of High Raise (2634 ft, 802 m) (8.6 miles: 13.8 km) passes a few yards west of the summit cairns.

Continue down to the col near Rampsgill Head and round above Twopenny Crag to the Straits of Riggindale, (GR.439122) where the bridleway to Hartsop leaves your route. *The way down to Hartsop is a rough ride with some treacherous bogs, but it is an 'emergency exit' from High Street, the only one for 14 miles (22 km)*

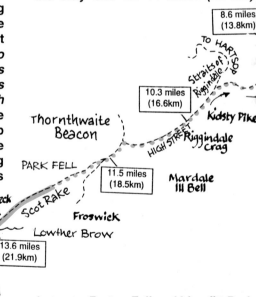

between Barton Fell and Limefitt Park. From here onwards the views are fantastic on a clear day, with Morecambe Bay visible far away to the south. Go along the ridge with the wall on your right for a few yards, and then through a gate. *Look out for Golden*

26

Eagles, whose only English nesting place is in Riggindale nearby. The bridleway continues with the wall a short distance away to the left, passing the summit of High Street (2718 feet, 828 m) (10.3 miles: 16.6 km).

From the summit, ride on southwards until you see the beacon, a 14 feet (4.25 m) stone column, at Thornthwaite Crag to the right (GR.432100). The

on this stretch. Half-way down you will have to divert uphill to avoid a three feet drop into a V-shaped gully.

Carry on down the track to meet a wall on your right. Ride beside it for a little way to a gate in the corner (GR.428080).

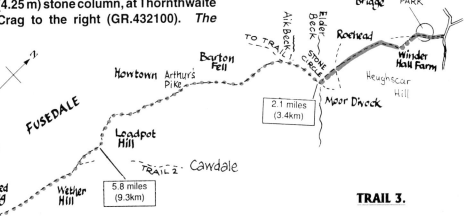

TRAIL 3.

ground is rocky and broken, and care is needed. Leaving the beacon on your right, you will see a Y-junction ahead, (GR.433095) (11.5 miles: 18.5 m). Your route bears off down the slope to the right, marked by a steel pole. The left-hand track is the footpath which goes along the ridge to Froswick and III Bell. The Ordnance Survey map marks your route as the line of the Roman road, but the footpath along the ridge is a more typically Roman route.

You are now on Scot Rake. The slope is gentle at first, but becomes very steep further down, about 1 in 2.5. A rider may choose to dismount and lead

Go through the gate and take the pleasant ride on a farm track. Continue until you come to two gates side-by-side, and take the left-hand one. Cross the stream (13.6 miles: 21.9 km), and ride to the left round a big pile of slate from the disused quarry nearby, and join the track near the stream, which is Hagg Gill.

Continue southwards along the track for another two miles (3.2 km), past Long Green Head Farm, to the bridleway junction (GR.418032), which leads down to Limefitt Park. Ride on along High Street, meeting the Garburn Road byway, a link with Trail 6, coming in from the left (16.0 miles: 25.8 km). A few yards on there is a Y-junction where you bear left on to the Longmire Road, a track which leads out on to the minor road at Allen Knott (GR.415012) and the end of your ride.

BAMPTON GRANGE TO LITTLE STRICKLAND

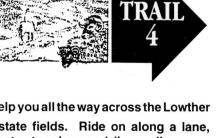

TRAIL 4

A 9 MILE (15 KM) CIRCULAR TRAIL (CLOCKWISE)

Ordnance Survey Map: The English Lakes NE Sheet (1:25,000)

Route: Bampton Grange - High Knipe - Burtree Bank - Little Strickland - Scarside

Parking & Starting Point: Your parking and starting point is at Bampton Grange (GR.523181)

Trail Grade: 1

Of Interest:
This is a pleasant easy ride, with little road work and no steep climbs or difficult terrain. It would be easy to start from Little Strickland if preferred, parking either in the village or between the A6 and the bridge over the motorway where there is a parking place.

Route Description:

Take the road eastwards from Bampton Grange and at the end of the village turn left along an unclassified road with grass verges and very little traffic. Go through the gate beside a cattle grid on to Knipe Moor and continue along the unfenced road, taking the first turn right at Howgate Foot. *From Knipe Moor you can see an interesting contrast between the white limestone rocks of Knipescar to the east and the older slaty rocks of the Lake District to the west.*

Climb up to High Knipe (1.2 miles: 1.9 km), turning right and then left in the farmyard - there are waymarks to

help you all the way across the Lowther Estate fields. Ride on along a lane, past a stone barn and diagonally across the next field to an iron gate, straight across the next field to a wicket gate, on past a stand of trees to the corner of a wire fence (GR.523206), where you turn right along the fence. *There is a handy trough where the horses can get a drink.*

Go through another wicket gate and straight across the next field up to Hill Plantation. *The track through the wood is rather rough but quite easy to follow.* When you come out of the wood, don't follow the wall on your left but go diagonally across to a farm gate. Cross the farm road and head uphill for the gate at the corner of the wood on Burtree Bank. Follow the good track along the side of the wood to a wicket gate on your left at the end. *This is a permissive bridleway which replaces one through the wood.* At two ash trees, bear right down hill to a bridge over Greenriggs Sike, then half-left to a gate in the corner on to an estate road. Cross the road and follow the sike round to an iron gate.

Ride through the cut in the wood and straight across the next field with the wood on your right. Go under the M6 (3.7 miles: 6.0 km) - *not as hairy as it sounds* - along the farm lane, and straight across the A6 - *take care crossing: there is little verge and although there is not much traffic it is pretty fast.*

28

Go half-right across the next field to a bridge across the railway. Over the bridge, turn right and go through a gate on your left into a wood. Follow a rather overgrown track to the right and look out for a stake painted orange on the left, which leads down to a footbridge over the River Leith. It is possible to ford the river to the left of the bridge. Ride straight on up the other side to a gate at the top, up the field to Sheriff Park, and through the gate at the right-hand corner. Keep straight on through three more gates on to a good track which leads to a farm lane and the road to Little Strickland, (GR.562198) (5.7 miles: 9.1 km). *The bridleway from Newby (Trail 14) joins a minor road half a mile north of the village.*

Ride through Little Strickland, which is a very attractive village, and turn right at the crossroads just beyond; go down Edge Brow, across the M6 and the railway until you reach the A6 again. Cross with great care, through the gate opposite on to a bridleway, turn right through another gate and diagonally across the next field to a wicket; straight on to a path through Shapbeck Plantation, continuing up the side of the wood to a high gate in a limestone wall. *A wonderful view spreads in front of you, with Haweswater gleaming between the fells.* Aim half-left downhill to a gate into a farm lane which takes you to Scarside (8.4 miles: 13.5 km) and on to a quiet road. Take the next turn right, (GR.535181), back to Bampton Grange a mile (1.6 km) away.

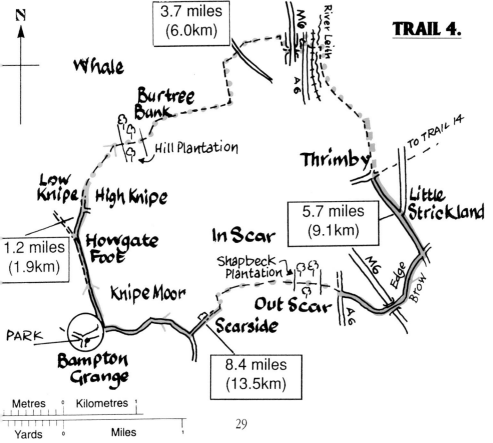

N

3.7 miles (6.0km)

TRAIL 4.

Whale

Burtree Bank

Hill Plantation

River Leith

M6

A6

Thrimby

TO TRAIL 14

Low Knipe

High Knipe

Little Strickland

In Scar

5.7 miles (9.1km)

1.2 miles (1.9km)

Howgate Foot

Shapbeck Plantation

M6

Edge Brow

Knipe Moor

Out Scar

A6

PARK

Scarside

Bampton Grange

8.4 miles (13.5km)

Metres   0   Kilometres

Yards   0   Miles

29

CODE FOR RIDING & DRIVING RESPONSIBLY

THE BRITISH
HORSE SOCIETY

1. **Riders and carriage drivers** everywhere should proceed with courtesy, care and consideration. The British Horse Society recommends the following:

    Care for the Land
    > Do not stray off the line of the path;
    > Do not damage timber or hedgerows by jumping;
    > Remember that horses' hooves can damage surfaces in bad weather;
    > Pay particular attention to protected areas that have significant historical and/or biological value, as they are extremely sensitive to damage.

    Courtesy to other users
    > Remember that walkers, cyclists and other riders may be elderly, disabled, children or simply frightened of horses; whenever possible acknowledge courtesy shown by drivers of motor vehicles.

    Consideration for the farmer
    > Shut the gate behind you;
    > Ride slowly past all stock;
    > Do not ride on cultivated land unless the right of way crosses it;
    > Dogs are seldom welcome on farmland or moorland unless on a lead or under close control.

2. **Observe local byelaws**

3. **Ride or drive with care on the roads** and take the BHS Riding and Road Safety Test. Always make sure that you can be seen at night or in bad visibility, by wearing the right kind of reflective/fluorescent aids.

4. **Groups from riding establishments** should contain reasonable numbers, for reasons of both safety and amenity. They should never exceed twenty in total **including** the relevant number of escorts as indicated in BHS guidelines on levels of capability among riders in groups, available on request. Rides should not deviate from the right of way or permitted route and regard must be shown at all times for growing crops, shutting and securing of gates and the consideration and courtesy due to others.

5. **Always obey the Country Code in every way possible:**
    > Enjoy the countryside and respect its life and work
    > Guard against all risk of fire
    > Fasten all gates
    > Keep your dogs under close control
    > Keep to public paths across farmland
    > Use gates and stiles to cross fences, hedges and walls
    > Leave livestock, crops and machinery alone
    > Take your litter home
    > Help keep all water clean
    > Protect wildlife, plants and trees
    > Take special care on country roads
    > Make no unnecessary noise.

GATESCARTH AND NAN BIELD PASSES

TRAIL 5

A 10 MILE (16 KM) CIRCULAR TRAIL (CLOCKWISE)

Ordnance Survey Map: The English Lakes SE Sheet (1:25,000)

Route: Mardale Head - Gatescarth Pass - Sadgill - Hallow Bank - Nan Bield Pass

Parking & Starting Point: Your parking and starting point is in the car park at Mardale Head (GR.469107). The car park may be busy during the tourist season, but there is no other parking accessible to this trail.

Trail Grade: 3. The going for part of this ride is very severe, over rocky, broken ground. Many riders would find their horses unsuitable for it. Nan Bield Pass is particularly difficult to negotiate. In emergency 4WD vehicles could not get on to the high ground on Gatescarth and Nan Bield Passes.

Of Interest:
The route is particularly scenic, with dramatic views over the surrounding fells. If the water level of the Haweswater reservoir is low you may see the remains of the flooded village of Mardale. The area is grazed by sheep: in the Haweswater catchment area they are Swaledale, whilst in Longsleddale Rough Fell sheep predominate. Both are hardy mountain breeds; in the Swaledale, both ewes and tups are horned, and they have a dark face with a mealy nose; the Rough Fell, found in the south-east of the Lake District, has a dark-coloured face often with patches of white.

ack horses with slate
om. Wrengill Quarry

31

Route Description:

Ride out from the car park and through the gate, and follow the bridleway to the left which runs along Gatescarth Beck. The path, signed for Longsleddale, is easy to see as it zig-zags up the fell. *To the right is Harter Fell, over which the Golden Eagles from Riggindale are sometimes to be seen.* The path crosses three streams, and care is needed on the second bridge.

Two miles (3.2 km) from Mardale Head the slope eases out and you reach a peaty area on Gatescarth Pass. Go through the gate in the wire fence (GR.474093). Take care on this section because parts of it are boggy. *The top of the pass is 1930 ft (590 m) above sea level.*

Follow Gatescarth Pass down to Brownhowe Bottom (GR.478085) on a rocky path down the fell, with stone steps towards the bottom. *On the right you will see the remains of Wrengill Quarry, which formerly produced fine quality Westmorland green roofing slate. In the early 18th century Wrengill was one of the first slates to be used on major buildings in the south of England. The slate was carried by packhorse nineteen miles to Milnthorpe, from where it went on by sea. The quarry was in full production for about 150 years; after that it was spasmodic, and finally closed more than 40 years ago. The bridleway from Trail 11 through Mosedale meets your route just south of the quarry, by the sheep pens.* Here you join the walled track which the quarry packhorses used, and follow it through an area of dramatic scree slopes and waterfalls as the River Sprint flows down the valley. *There are some very sharp zig-zags which the track*

follows, with its walls. The track is stone pitched in places and may be slippery when wet.

When you reach the metalled road, turn right over the bridge towards the farms at Sadgill, (GR.483057) (3.6 miles: 5.8 km). There is a barn on your right where the road turns left towards a farm. Go through the gate, and the

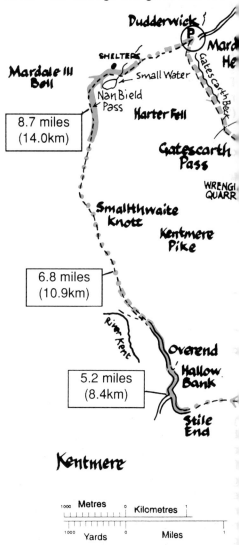

Kentmere

Metres	Kilometres

Yards	Miles

byway sign directs you to the right past the buildings.

Follow the walled track, with mixed woodland on either side, until you reach a gate by the ruins of a field house. The track goes along the wall to another gate where there is a signpost. Take the byway to the right and up the hill, signed Kentmere and High Lane. *(The bridleway to the south joins Trail 6). This path takes you over open land dotted with hawthorn trees, and grazed by sheep and ponies.* Go through a gate at the old farm buildings at Stile End, then down a walled track to a metalled road, High Lane, (GR.465050) (5.2 miles: 8.4 km).

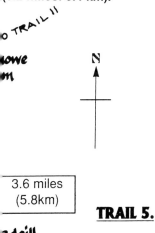

```
o TRAIL ''
lowe          N
m             ↑
              |
        ——————+——————
              |
              |
┌──────────────┐
│  3.6 miles   │
│  (5.8km)     │     TRAIL 5.
└──────────────┘
adgill
```

Turn right and follow the road for 200 yards (180 m), then turn left to take the bridleway to Mardale. Go through another gate and head towards the farm - the bridleway goes through the gate to the right of the farm. After a short distance you reach the metalled road again, with three gates across the road at Hallow Bank to make sheep pens, so care will be needed at certain times of the year.

At Overend (GR.464058) the bridleway bears right and runs roughly parallel to the footpath. The track crosses a series of fords across the becks from Kentmere Pike which drain into the River Kent - at two there are waterfalls. To reach the fell gate you have to ford the beck (GR.456070) (6.8 miles: 10.9km).

Once on the open fell the path begins to climb fairly steeply. The plateau is wet and peaty. The path follows the contour round Smallthwaite Knott, then climbs steadily, crossing about nine becks on the way to the foot of Nan Bield Pass. *From here you see Harter Fell on your right and Mardale III Bell to the left.*

The cairned path up to Nan Bield is steep and stony. At the top, at 2100 ft (640 m) (8.7 miles: 14.0 km), there is a shelter where the paths form a crossroads. *On most passes there is a level stretch on the col; but at Nan Bield the bridleway crosses a ridge, so that the descent starts abruptly.* Go straight on down towards Small Water, on a path which is very steep and stony, and needs great care. It is one of those places where you might be wise to dismount and lead. The path descends to go round the northern side of Small Water. Near the tarn you pass three slate shelters. From here the path rises gently, then drops again to cross the Small Water Beck (GR.457101).

The bridleway continues down towards Haweswater, passing through a wicket gate (GR.461104) where you have to go carefully because there is a steep step down. The path takes you past sheep folds back to the car park at Mardale Head.

STAVELEY TO KENTMERE

TRAIL 6

A 29 MILE (47 km) FIGURE OF EIGHT TRAIL (ANTI-CLOCKWISE FIRST)

Ordnance Survey Map: The English Lakes SE Sheet (1:25,000)

Route: Staveley - Braban House - Longsleddale - Cocklaw Fell - Kentmere - High House - Moor Howe - Dubbs Road - Garburn Road - Kentmere again - Long Houses - Park House - Hall Lane.

Parking & Starting Point: Parking is available in a cul-de-sac at the western end of Staveley bypass on the line of the old road (GR.461984). There are very few other suitable parking places on the whole of this trail, although you could find somewhere to load along Moor Howe Road or Potter Fell Road. The roads up Kentmere and Longsleddale valleys are very narrow with frequent blind corners: not recommended for horse transport.

Trail Grade: From 1 to 3 as given below:
Grade 1: Kentdale and Longsleddale - a pleasant ride mainly near the valley bottom.
Grade 2: Kentmere Park to Dubbs Road - a few soft places around Park Beck, otherwise easy going.
Grade 2: Kentmere and Staveley Head Fell.
Grade 3: Cocklaw Fell - soft going in places and the risk of mist are hazards. Accurate map reading is required.
Grade 3: Garburn Pass - a very rocky, broken surface.
This route would not be accessible to emergency vehicles between Till's Hole (GR.483051) and Cornclose Lane (GR.462036); or on the Garburn Road (GR.423037 to GR.453045) even though it is a byway.

Of Interest:
Longsleddale and Kentmere are two of the smaller valleys carved out by the southbound glaciers flowing off the dome of what is now the Lake District. When the ice began to retreat some 10,000 years ago, the valleys emerged and filled with lakes where they were dammed with glacial debris. The gradual erosion of these barriers, combined with silting of the lake floors, has reduced the area of open water remaining. In both dales, flat fields in the valley bottoms indicate the final stage of silting, leaving only a river in Longsleddale and a narrow reed-grown tarn in Kentmere. Steep rocky dale sides contrast with both the flat bottom land and the more waterlogged, peaty expanses of the watersheds above.

These physical conditions have influenced the use made of the area by plant and animal life and by Man. Thus the fertile silts of the valleys, which are level enough to be mown, are used as meadows, and the hillside as grazing for cattle and sheep; whereas the peaty watersheds are more suited to hill sheep only. When Man first settled here the valley bottoms would have been very wet and choked with trees: it was therefore easier with primitive tools to clear the more lightly wooded and better drained hillsides. Only as population increased and tools improved would the dale bottoms have been exploited and grazing extended on to the watersheds.

The vegetation pattern we see now is therefore the effect of husbandry on natural development. Native woods, as distinct from some new conifer plantations, are now mainly confined to steep rocky areas; the contraction of woodland has been accelerated through historic times by sheep grazing preventing the growth of young trees. In the past half century there has been a similar reduction in the area of heather moorland which gives way to grass-sedge and bracken in the face of heavier grazing.

Animal wildlife also takes what advantage it can of prevailing conditions. On dry, steep pastures, notably at the foot of Longsleddale, you may see turf dug up by badgers in search of cockchafer grubs, whereas buzzards and kestrels sail and hover over rougher ground which harbours voles and other prey. Birds dependent on water congregate on the tarn in Kentmere, while Skeggles Water, seen to the south from the route over Cocklaw Fell, is an important staging post for migrant birds. Green Woodpeckers, Jays and Magpies are conspicuous in the dale-side woods, and you may be lucky enough to see a Red Squirrel in the old coppice woods near Staveley.

One can gain an indication of farming trends from buildings and field walls. In Kentmere, for example, there is an intricate pattern of small irregular fields above which are the large, straight-walled 'allotments' mainly of the 18th Century enclosure awards. Many of these walls have fallen into disrepair, but an increasing number of being restored.

Route Description:

Kentdale: From the lay-by ride eastwards towards the village for a quarter of a mile (400m) and turn left on to Brow Lane, which leads to a T-junction by the church where you turn left, then right across Barley Bridge and immediately right · again, signed Burneside. This is a narrow road, but it has very little traffic. Take the first turning to the left and ride up the hill past Craggy Plantation.

Turn right immediately before the gate (GR.482989) and go up the byway, with the wall on your left, to a gate at the top of the hill leading into a narrow green lane between stone walls. It goes on through the wood called Spring Hag to arrive at a minor road where you turn right and ride down the hill to another road where you turn left and go along beside the River Kent for about half a mile (0.8 km).

Turn left up the Hundhowe farm track at GR.493978 (3.0 miles: 4.8 km) and ride up past the farm to a gate at the end of the big barn which leads into a narrow track between stone walls. On the crest of the hill bear right and go down the track beside the beck which leads out on to the road again at Mirefoot, where you turn right. 220 yards (200 m) along turn left, just before the sharp bend, into a green lane which leads into a field near Braban House. Bear left across the field, go through the right-hand gate, and leave the house on your right; bear left on to a track which leads out to a T-junction, where you turn left towards a field gate. Bear left in the field and ride up the hill to a ruined building, through the left-hand gateway and turn right, to ride on with the long straight wall on your right. Opposite a small stand of trees the wall bears away to the right but you continue across the open field to another wall which comes up from the wood, and ride on with that wall on your left to a bridleway gate. Ride

through the next three fields, with the wall on your right, to the road to Beetham Bank, where you turn left.

Ride up the hill and bear left, behind the buildings, on to a track across the field which bears right and leads to a narrow green lane between hedges. Turn right to ride down to Shepherds Green, then left to leave the buildings on your right and continue up the lane to Potter Fell Road, where you turn right. Turn left at the T-junction, and ride on towards Garnett Bridge.

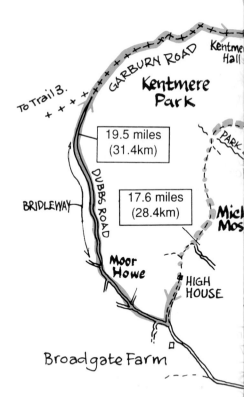

Longsleddale: Leave the road a quarter of a mile (0.4 km) south of Garnett Bridge at GR.522988 where there is a bridleway sign on the left for Sadgill, not easily seen among the trees (6.0 miles; 9.7 km). Through the gate and turn right, and ride along a grass track which keeps fairly close to the road. Bear left at the Y-junction. Go through the gateway in the next wall and bear slightly right across the field. Across the next field bear left towards an outcrop of rock just below the wood and aim for the far right-hand corner of the field, where the bridleway leads out on to a lonning. Cross it and follow the bridleway sign towards Nether House Farm, on a grass track along the contour.

At GR.521995 the track leads into another lonning which turns right very soon, but you go straight on through a bridleway gate into the next field, bear right and ride up the hill towards a belt of woodland, to arrive at a gate in the far right-hand corner.

In the next field keep the wall on your right, then through a gate and continue with the wall on your left, leading to a gate out on to the farm road., At Nether House Farm leave the buildings on your left and bear right across the next field on a grass track. Follow the track past Tenter Howe, which is a ruin, and on to Bridge End.

Bear right and ride along the bank of the River Sprint for 600 yards (550 m) to the end of the field, turn left and go through a gate on the right on to the track to Docker Nook. *The bridleway to the right is the link with Trail 7.* Just before the

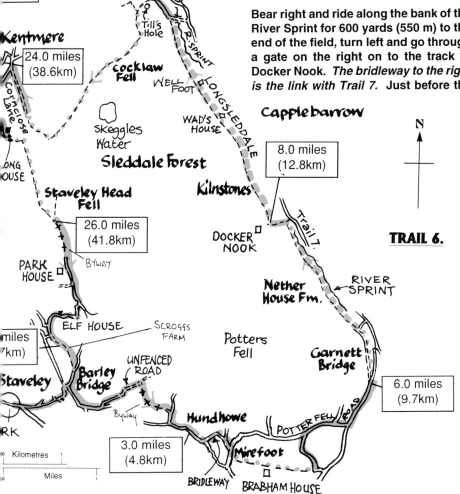

37

farm turn sharp right at a bridleway signpost (8.0 miles: 12.8 km) towards the corner of the field where there are two gates; take the right-hand one. The grass track continues across the next three fields round the foot of Dockernook Wood towards Kilnstones, where you pass between the house and the barn to cross a flagged bridge across the beck. Ride on across the next three fields with the wall on your left until you come to two gates at GR.501027. Take the left-hand one and continue with the wall on your right past the next farm and across a small field.

In the next field bear right down the bank to join a turf-covered track which crosses four fields and a beck bridge to arrive at Wad's Howe Farm. Here turn right in the yard and go through the gate; 50 yards (45 m) down the lane, turn left into a field and ride along the top on a grass track, on to Hollin Root which you leave on your left. The track, easily discernible, continues across the next field to Well Foot, where there is a diversion to the left to avoid the farm buildings. Rejoin the track and ride, with the fence on your right, past Hill Cottage and on to join the farm road to Tom's Howe; there go through a gate on the right just before the yard, down the hill with the wall on your right to join the farm road to Till's Hole, and turn left at GR.485052 (11.0 miles: 17.8 km).

The bridleway above Till's Hole is steep and stony; near the top the wall on your right bears away and there you turn left and ford the little beck. Bear right, up the hill, to a gate in the wall at the top which leads on to a track. Here you turn left; *the bridleway to the right is the link with Trail 5.*

In the next field the track starts to fade away; ride southwards until you come to a ruined wall, turn right and ride along its near side to a gate at the top which leads

on to Cocklaw Fell. Here the route cannot be seen on the ground and there are large boggy tracts. Keep to the right to avoid them, not far from the right-hand wall; and, once you have gained sufficient height, aim for the gate by the wall junction (GR.477040). The bearing from gate to gate across Cocklaw Fell is 236 degrees.

Kentmere: From here on the track across successive enclosures down towards Kentmere becomes gradually more apparent, leading into Cornclose Lane and so down to the road at GR.461040. Here turn left down Lowfield Lane, ride down the steep hill and turn sharp right towards Kentmere. *This is an awkward narrow road with considerable tourist traffic, but it is less than half a mile to Kentmere church.*

At the church (14.7 miles: 23.6 km) take the farm track on the left, a bridleway, down to Kentmere Hall. The farm buildings, on your right, include a 14th Century pele tower, now ruinous, and a 15th Century house which was the birthplace in 1517 of Bernard Gilpin, the evangelist known as 'the Apostle of the North'.*

Turn left as you reach the yard and go through a waymarked field gate. Ride uphill on a hard track; keep straight on alongside the wood, don't bear left into it. At the end of the wood, go out on to the open fell and ride southwards on the hard track with the wall on your left. The track swings west to arrive at a gate with Park Beck immediately beyond, (GR.443027). Turn left and ride along the beck side for about 150 yards (135 m) and ford it opposite the outcrop. The bridleway, now much less clear and rather wet in places, goes just to the left of a group of three Rowan trees and on to a gate in the corner between two walls.

Turn left and ride southwards with the wall on your left to a gate which leads into a grass track between stone walls, for a short distance. The track continues beside Mickle Moss and you go on, with the wall on your right, to a gate (GR.440009) (17.6 miles: 28.4 km).

Through the gate there is a T-junction where you turn sharp right into a field; the track swings left to a cross-roads where you turn left to a gate beside a big Ash tree; down the next field with the wall on your left to High House Farm. Ride between the buildings on a cobbled track, turn left, and on to join the minor road (GR.435096), where you turn right.

Garburn Pass: *This road has little traffic. After a mile (1.6 m) turn right at Moor Howe (GR.423006) on to the Dubbs Road, which is a bridleway, a hard track between stone walls. After a mile and a half (2.5km) you join the Garburn Road, a byway which is the route to Kentmere (19.5 miles: 31.4 km). The track from the left is the link with High Street, Trail 3. From here on the track becomes increasingly stony: it is not impassable but there are several places which are very awkward, where it may be necessary to dismount and lead.*

The Garburn Road was formerly part of the drove road for cattle from West Cumberland, going across to Longsleddale and then on to join the main route to the markets in the south of England.

Kentmere: As you approach Kentmere village, at GR.451045, take the right-hand fork, which is the byway; ride down to the minor road, and turn left to go down to Kentmere church (24.0 miles: 38.6 km). From the church, ride down the road for three-quarters of a mile (1.2 km). *The road is very narrow and has considerable tourist traffic, so great care is needed.* At Long Houses (GR.458031) turn left on to the bridleway, signed for Staveley Head. Ride up the track and turn right to go between the buildings. *On the farmhouse on the left there is a fine plaque in the*

plaster inscribed: F The style is more usually seen as a marriage lintol, W D the top letter being the initial of the couple's 1703 surname, the lower letters those of their Christian names, and the date the year of their marriage. Such inscriptions, dating usually from the late 17th to the early 19th Century, are quite often to be seen on Cumbrian farmhouses.

Ride up the hill on a hard track between stone walls; near the top there are two gates and the bridleway, waymarked, it through the left-hand one. This leads across open ground to a Y-junction where you take the right-hand fork. Across the Nuttera Beck you ride on with the wall on your right, on a track in the turf. When the wall bears away to the right keep going straight on, past a waymark post a hundred yards ahead. This leads to a bridleway crossroads half a mile (0.8 km) away, where you go through the gate opposite and bear left to a gate in the far left corner of the field, beyond which there is a T-junction, at GR.469015 (26.0 miles: 41.8 km).

Staveley: Turn right on to the byway, which is a hard track, and ride down the hill to Park House to join the minor road. Half a mile (0.8 km) further on, turn right into a field, on a bridleway signed to Elfhowe. Follow the beck down the hill, and cross the bridge into a green lane between stone walls, which leads to Elfhowe and then on to a short minor road. You join the Kentmere road, then leave it immediately on a bridleway to the left, a narrow track leading to Scroggs Farm (27.8 miles: 44.7 km), from where the farm road goes down to Hall Lane, and you ride on to cross the River Kent at Barley Bridge.

Over the bridge and turn left, and the first turning on the right is Brown Lane, which takes you back to the starting point.

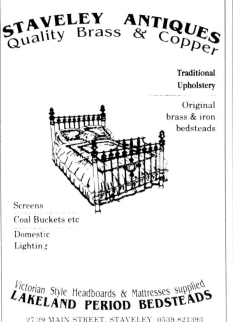

REDFERN HORSEWEAR

Designers and makers of attractive, tough and hardwearing:-

TRAVEL BOOTS, BRUSHING BOOTS AND KNEE BOOTS, WOOL-FLEECE NUMNAHS, SADDLE-BAGS AND TAIL GUARDS

Obtainable locally from:

Slack's Equestrian Supplies
White Stone
Newby, Penrith
Telephone: 0931 714375

and

The Saddlers
15 Little Dockray
Penrith
Telephone: 0768 62363

The Saddlers
(C. & J. K. Armstrong)

Quality Saddlery . Riding Wear
Leather Gifts . Sticks . Travel Goods
All at Competitive Prices

15 Little Dockray, Penrith,
Cumbria, CA11 7HL
Tel. & Fax. 0768 62363

General information about accommodation is always available from the:

**Cumbria Tourist Board,
Ashleigh, Holly Road,
Windermere, Cumbria
LA23 2AQ.
Telephone: 05394 44444**

LONGSLEDDALE TO SHAP

TRAIL 7

The Stage Coach at Hause Foot

AN 8 MILE (13 KM) LINK
LINEAR ROUTE - NORTHWARDS

Ordnance Survey Map: The English Lakes SE Sheet (1:25,000)

Route: Longsleddale - Plough Farm - Bannisdale High Bridge - Wolf Howe - Hollowgate - High Borrow Bridge - Hause Foot - Packhorse Hill - Wasdale Old Bridge

Parking & Starting Point: There is no parking place near the start of this route, which is included here only as a link between Trails 6, 8, and 10. There is room for one horse box on the verge (GR.530999). At the other end there is parking space by the A6 (GR.565087).

Trail Grade: 2. Much of the way is easy riding, but there are some boggy places on Shap Fell, and mist is also a hazard there.

Of Interest:

For most of its course this link follows the turnpike road which was built in the 1750's. It is unusual because it is one of the few turnpikes in the country which has not been swept away by later highway construction on the same route. It survives because it was superseded by a new turnpike, opened in 1822, which was on the line now followed by the A6. This link then fell into disuse, but it is still passable.

42

The route follows the approximate line of an ancient medieval track, known as the 'magna strata'. However, by the 18th century any carriageway which there might have been had disappeared, and the route actually used extended in some places to several hundred yards wide as travellers struggled to find their way across desolate and often featureless country.

This was the state at the time of the '45 Rebellion, when both armies suffered serious transport problems. The retreating Highlanders struggled back towards Scotland on this route, while the Duke of Cumberland's army went an easier but much longer way through Orton, to head them off at Clifton Moor, south of Penrith. There on 17th December 1745 a minor engagement between the two armies was the last battle ever to be fought on English soil.

These problems made the authorities realise that a good road was urgently needed. Accordingly, the Heron Syke to Eamont Bridge Turnpike Trust was established by Act of Parliament in 1753 for the construction of a new road from the Lancashire boundary 36 miles northwards across Westmorland.

This turnpike was a properly engineered highway 20 feet wide, with the central third paved, enabling wheeled traffic to travel on the route for the first time. It was the M6 of its day: the Flying Machine, a stage coach drawn by six horses which began a service from Carlisle to London in 1763, did that journey in the incredibly fast time of three days, driving over Shap Fells on this turnpike at five to six miles an hour. Although a fast coach, it was not generally popular: 'there was a long coach, shaped like a boat, which would hold about a dozen persons inside, while perhaps a like number might get upon the roof. This heavy lumbering vehicle...'

The route was described as 'exceedingly hilly and sometimes very steep, but the road itself excellent'. The turnpike is clearly and accurately shown on Thomas Jefferys's map of Westmorland at the scale of one inch to one mile, surveyed in 1768.

The road was replaced in 1822 by another turnpike, with easier gradients, designed by John Loudon Macadam and following the line of what is now the A6. Both routes are shown on Orlando Hodgson's map, published in 1828. (Illustration overleaf).

Route Description:

Leave the Longsleddale bridleway where it meets the road (GR.509015) and turn right, on to a minor road which is very narrow and twisting, where care is needed. After half a mile (0.8 km) turn left at Murthwaite Farm (GR.514007). Ride up the yard, through a gate at the top, and bear right on a steep stony track. This track crosses two fields and then fades out. Bear left and aim for the top of the wood, where there is a bridleway gate. In the next field bear left and follow the marker posts to a gate in the far corner, then along a track between stone walls. At GR.524005 turn right on to another track which leads down to a minor road at Mosergh Farm. Turn left, go on to join the turnpike (GR.530998) (1.9 miles: 3.0 km), and turn left.

Ride northwards along a narrow road bounded by stone walls which date apparently from later in the century when this area was enclosed. *Plough Farm, on your right (GR.532002), now a modern bungalow, is the site of a coaching inn later replaced by the Plough Inn nearby on the A6.*

43

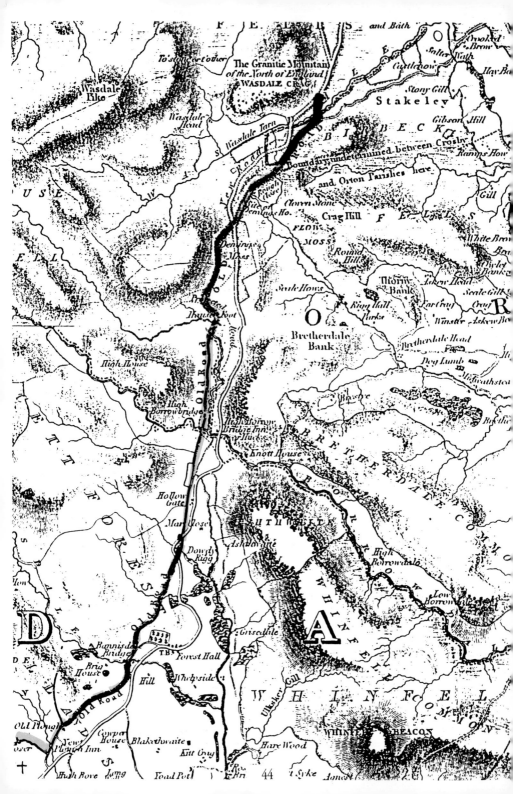

The road swings sharp left, but on the corner opposite there is a field gate signed Public Bridleway, and this is your route. *The turnpike swings away across the field in a shallow S bend through a cutting. For the next two miles (3.2 km) it can be seen as a 20 feet wide swathe across the fells, forming a berm excavated on the upper side and filled on the lower. In certain places it looks narrower, but this is because a wall has been built later within the width of the turnpike.*

At GR.537006 there is an old water trough behind the wall on your left which, from its position, is likely to have been built to serve the turnpike. After passing a small wood on the right, you cross a driveway and ride down the hill to join a minor road. *There is another old water trough just before the gate.*

Turn left, and go down to Bannisdale High Bridge, which was the site of a turnpike gate. Continuing up the hill, there is a gate on the left just past Thorn Cottage, and you turn in there (GR.542013) (3.1 miles: 5.0 km). *For the next mile, to the 'Jungle', the way is a track of turf with a hard foundation.*

You rejoin the A6 at the 'Jungle'.(the caravan sales area is so called because before the M6 was opened it was the site of the Jungle Cafe, a well-known pull-up for lorry drivers). Here you can either ride along the main road for 250 yards (230m) or cross on to the wide verge and then re-cross. Either is reasonable if you take care because the A6 is not generally heavily trafficked.

Turn left (GR.548027) on to a minor road with very little traffic, going up past Hollowgate and then down to High Borrow Bridge (5.0 miles: 8.1 km). *This bridge has been built in two parts, having a four foot wide extension on the east side to make it wider. It was probably on old packhorse bridge which was widened to accommodate the turnpike traffic.* The road continues to Hause Foot in Crookdale, formerly a coaching inn and recently restored as a private house.

From here you can see the wisdom of Macadam's design for the 1822 diversion. Across the valley to your right, the A6 climbs steadily to the summit at an average gradient of 1 in 16. By contrast, your route on the old turnpike has gained height only slightly since High Borrow Bridge, but ahead you have three-quarters of a mile (1.2 km) to the summit at an average gradient of 1 in 10, and much steeper in places. It must have been a real struggle for six horses drawing a coach with 24 passengers at five miles an hour. It is not surprising that a passenger had to pay a heavy surcharge if he had more than 10lbs (4.8 kilos) weight of luggage.

At Hause Foot, ride across the yard, through a gateway and up a very rocky track where the going is quite difficult. *This is the present line of the public byway, but the turnpike actually went across the field on your left. You rejoin it after going through the next gate.* On the fell the turnpike swings round to the right and rises to another gate (GR.547059). From here for the next half a mile the route is wet in places and care is needed, but it should be passable

Cross the A6 (6.9 miles: 11.1 km) and continue north-eastwards along the turnpike which can be clearly seen. *A*

45

few yards along, on your right, there is one of its original milestones, marking ten miles from Kendal. Half a mile (0.8km) farther on, the hill on your left called Packhorse Hill was probably a landmark in pre-turnpike days. Looking half-left past Packhorse Hill you see the face of the Shap Pink Granite quarry, on the site marked on Hodgson's map as 'The Granitic Mountain of the North of England'.

At GR.559076 you pass the junction with the bridleway which leads to Ewelock Bank (Trail 10), then go through a gate and down a hard track by the wood. A mile away half-right you can see the buildings of the Shap Wells Hotel, which was built as a spa in the 1830's, and during the Second World War was a prisoner-of-war camp

for German generals. Immediately south of Wasdale Old Bridge the Trail 10 bridleway comes in from the north-east, and this link ends there. The turnpike route continues northwards for another one and three quarter miles (3.0 km) and then rejoins the A6.

Deer hunting

FOLLOWING A ROUTE

The descriptions given in this book were correct at the time of printing but it should be borne in mind that landmarks and conditions can change. It is assumed every user will carry and be competent in the use of the appropriate Ordnance Survey Pathfinder or Landranger map. This is essential as the route may not be waymarked along the whole of its length.

TRAIL
8

A 16 MILE (26 KM) CIRCULAR TRAIL (CLOCKWISE)

Ordnance Survey Map: The English Lakes SE Sheet (1:25,000)

Route: Bannisdale High Bridge - Borrowdale - Whinfell - Watchgate - Murthwaite - Plough Farm

Parking & Starting Point: There is a good parking place on the east side of the road, just south of Bannisdale High Bridge, on a loop of the old turnpike (GR.541011), and this is your starting point.

Trail Grade: 2.

Of Interest:
This route makes a wide circuit round Whinfell Beacon (1548 ft, 472 m) which, according to Wainwright, is one of a system of beacons set up in the Border counties to give warning of Scottish invaders. It was probably established early in the 15th Century. The hill was described in a 19th Century directory as 'a lofty conical eminence'.

Route Description:

Ride north over Bannisdale High Bridge. Just beyond Thorn Cottage there is a bridleway sign on the left. Go through the gate and follow the old road, which climbs as a cart-track round a wall corner. It continues climbing and then gently descends, always with the wall on the right, to reach the A6.

Cross, with care, straight over the A6 on to the old road and turn right through the two gates beside the cattle grid, and ride down the road towards Ashstead Farm. Just before the farm

turn sharp left through a gate which leads on to the fell and follow the track, a byway, which gradually rises until it reaches the A6 again. Turn right immediately before the gate and ride up the hill, near the fence of the main road; this is not a public right of way, but the owner kindly allows access; please take particular care. In 200 yards (180 m) you go through a gate (2.2 miles: 3.6km) and join a track on the right, a byway, which leads down into Borrowdale.

Ride for a mile on the track, which is here a bridleway, along the south side of the Borrow Beck, and cross by the bridge. Continue through the fields, passing the ruins of High Borrowdale on your left. Low Borrowdale, half a mile (0.8 km) further on (4.3 miles: 6.9km), is still a working farm. Ride straight through the yard and continue along the clear track which crosses the beck by another bridge (GR.588011). Just before the next cattle grid, (GR.594014) (5.6 miles: 9.0 km), turn right uphill on a track.

Ride quite steeply uphill through the trees and then out on to open ground. The track leads to a gate from which two masts are clearly visible. *The left-hand mast belongs to Mercury and the one on the right to British Telecom.* Go through the gate and continue on the track which leads to the BT mast. Join the unfenced tarmac road and follow it downhill. *It is a bridleway which has been paved to give vehicles access to the masts in all weathers.*

The next part of the trail goes through a delightful series of narrow country lanes and byways to bring you to the A6. *Follow the map and directions carefully as there are virtually no signposts, and the route is designed to bring you out at a point where you can cross straight over the A6.*

When you reach the public road (GR.569982) (8.3 miles: 13.4 km) turn right and ride for a mile, going straight ahead at one crossroads and passing a No Through Road sign as the road curves sharply left. At the T-junction go straight ahead on to the stony track leading down to Guestford Farm. Ride past the farm and across two fields to the River Mint. Cross by the ford and continue on the track with the hedge on your right until you reach the road (GR.552993).

TRAIL 8.

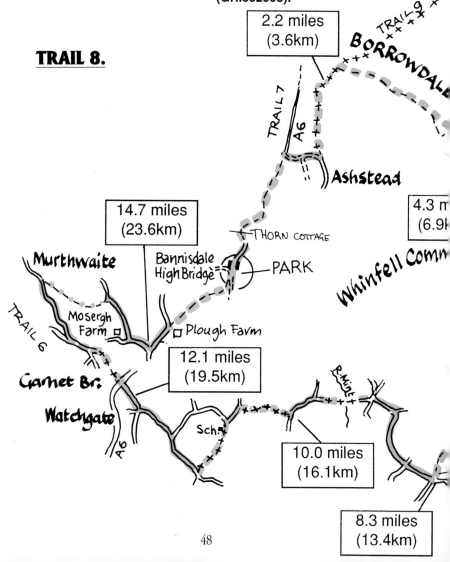

2.2 miles (3.6km)

14.7 miles (23.6km)

4.3 m (6.9k

12.1 miles (19.5km)

10.0 miles (16.1km)

8.3 miles (13.4km)

Turn left, ride uphill for a quarter of a mile (0.4 km), and turn sharp right (GR.549990) (10.0 miles: 16.1 km) into a stony walled lane. When you reach the road leading to Candy Slack Farm turn left, and at the next junction turn left again and ride past Selside School.

Follow the track across three fields until the next road is reached (GR.537982). Turn right and ride for three quarters of a mile (1.2 km), passing one turning on the right. At Watchgate turn right, and when you meet the A6 (12.1 miles: 19.5 km) ride straight across with care into the walled lane which is marked as a bridleway.

Ride downhill: the track goes through a gate and continues downhill through pastures and then into another walled lane until it reaches the road up Longsleddale valley. This road is narrow and winding, so be on the look-out for traffic. Ride north-westwards on this road for just over half a mile (1.0 km) until you reach Murthwaite Farm. Turn right and ride up through the farmyard and through a gate ahead on to a track which climbs steeply uphill. When the track peters out ride across the field to the top corner of a small conifer plantation and go through the waymarked gate. Turn left and head towards the broken wall. Ride uphill with the wall on your right at first and follow two waymark posts which take you to another marked gate (GR.522004) through into a walled track. Turn right at the T-junction and ride down to Mosergh Farm. Turn left at the road and left again at the T-junction (14.7 miles: 23.6 km) to ride up to Plough Farm.

Go through the gate on the right with a bridleway sign and follow the clear grassy track. *This is the old road into Scotland used by pack-horse trains long before the A6 was built.* The old road ascends gently, passing through gated fields on a raised causeway before descending to cross the driveway to Lowbridge House. It goes through a patch of woodland to reach the road and your starting point.

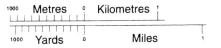

1000 Metres 0 Kilometres 1

1000 Yards 0 Miles 1

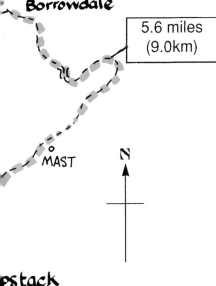

'owdale

Low
Borrowdale

5.6 miles
(9.0km)

MAST

N

pstack

A 9 MILE (15 KM) CIRCULAR TRAIL (CLOCKWISE)

Ordnance Survey Maps:
Sheet NY60/70 & The English Lakes SE Sheet (1:25,000)

Route: Roundthwaite - Birk Knott - Belt Howe - Borrowdale - Breasthigh Road - Midwath Stead - Greenholme - Pikestone Lane

Parking & Starting Point: Parking is available beside the bridleway access, just south of Roundthwaite, your starting point at GR.609033.

Trail Grade: 2. Although the mileage of this circuit is quite short most of it is over fell tracks and involves some steep ascents and descents.

Hill shepherding

Route Description:

From your parking place take the bridleway heading south-west up on to the fell. Continue along the track keeping the wall on your right. When that wall ends (GR.600026) continue on the track up the valley. Cross the stream and at GR.595025 bear left uphill with the stream in the valley on your left. The track is now less distinct; keep heading west. At the head of the small valley the path bears left and crosses a patch of rushes and becomes more distinct again (GR.590025). Continue uphill and after 200 yards (180 m) there is a small outcrop of sharp rocks on the right. At this point, GR.588023, turn sharp left uphill away from the track, and shortly you will pick up a grassy track which soon slopes down into a rush-filled gully and then climbs gently again. The going is safe but there is only a sheep track to follow. Ride on to the head of the gully with the rushes on your left and you will join the well-defined path (GR.587022) leading down into Borrowdale.

Low Borrowdale Farm is ahead, surrounded by trees. When you get down to the farm (2.2 miles: 3.6 km) turn right on a good track. After crossing two fields you will pass High Borrowdale Farm which is a ruin on your right, and the track continues across fields to reach the Borrow Beck which is crossed by a bridge at GR.569030. Ride along the south bank of the beck until the track turns away to go uphill. At this

50

point (GR.555037) turn right and cross the beck by a ford (4.1 miles: 6.6 km), going through the gate and following the rutted track uphill.

You have now joined a byway, *the Breasthigh Road, so called because it goes over the breast of the hill down into Bretherdale. At the top of the hill there is a marvellous view over the broad Eden valley to the distant Pennines.* After descending a short way you will see a barn on your right. Join the track leading away from it which crosses the Breasthigh Beck. Continue downhill on the track and after about 200 yards (180 m) re-cross the beck at a ford, thus avoiding a very stony area. Follow the track downhill into a short walled lane (GR.575049).

At the metalled road turn right and ride down to Midwath Stead Farm (6.3 miles: 10.1 km). Cross the Bretherdale Beck and ride uphill on the road, which is unfenced on one side. At the top of the hill, at GR.588050, turn right on to a track going uphill and go through the left-hand of two gates. Follow the track, which descends gently towards a small clump of trees. Cross over the path leading to a derelict farmhouse on the left. Go through an iron gate and ride downhill to Low Whinnowe Farm; through the gate, keeping the farm buildings on your right, and join the track which leads to Greenholme.

At Greenholme, GR.598058, turn right on to the road signed Tebay and Kendal and ride for two miles along Pikestone Lane, a quiet country road, until you reach the hamlet of Roundthwaite, and your parking place.

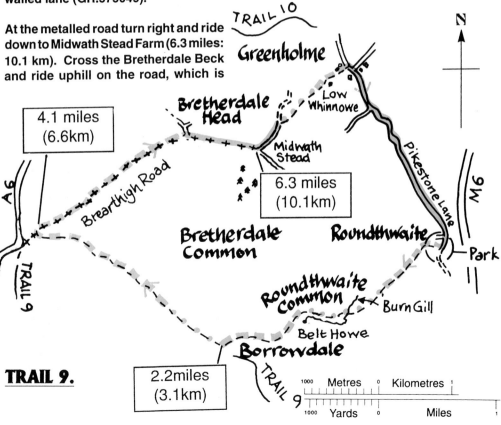

4.1 miles (6.6km)

6.3 miles (10.1km)

TRAIL 9.

2.2miles (3.1km)

BIRKBECK FELLS

TRAIL 10

A 10 MILE (16 KM) CIRCULAR TRAIL (ANTI-CLOCKWISE)

Ordnance Survey Maps: The English Lakes SE Sheet & Sheet NY60/70 (1:25,000)

Route: Thunder Stone - Salterwath - Wasdale Old Bridge - Packhorse Hill - Birkbeck Fells - Ewelock Bank - Scout Green - Sproat Ghyil

Parking & Starting Point: Park on the turf beside the B6261 just west of the cattle grid which is two miles (3.2 km) north-west of Orton (GR.600091)

Trail Grade: 2. The going is not difficult on this ride, but it does include some featureless country where good map-reading is essential, and which should be avoided in the mist.

Route Description:

Ride north-westwards along the unfenced road and cross under the M6 by two separate bridges. After the second take the first turning to the left and go down an unfenced road, and under the railway to Salterwath (the "salt dealers' ford") (1.6 miles: 2.6 km). Leave the farm on your left, go on towards the beck and take the track to the left. Ride across the bridge, through the gate, turn left, and after a few yards turn right and ride up the hill on to the fell with the wall on your right. Follow the wall when it swings to the right until you come to a gas marker post. Here turn left, leave the line of the wall, and aim across country towards the left-hand edge of the wood a quarter of a mile (400 m) ahead.

The bridleway is a track through the heather, rather wet in places but with a hard base. Because of heavy grazing by sheep, heather moor is becoming a relatively scarce feature. Here it is in good condition, being protected from over-grazing in the interests of grouse, whose main food is heather. Shooting butts can be seen in the distance.

One and a half miles (2.4 km) after leaving Salterwath you meet the turn-pike, a byway, (GR.565083), just above Wasdale Old Bridge. Turn left and ride up the hill on a broad track beside the wood, through a gate and out on to the fell.120 yards (110 m) south of the wood, approaching Packhorse Hill, you turn left off the turnpike (GR.559076) (3.6 miles: 5.8 km). The bridleway is on a good track to start with, but this eventually fades out. At GR.563071 you will see a post ahead marking a gas pipeline; here swing round sharply to the left on a less distinct track. Ride towards the knoll which carries the cairn on Crag Hill, turn sharp left at its foot and soon turn right, skirting a small bog. Passing Crag Hill on your right you soon pick up a faint grass track leading south-east towards Nan Hill. At GR.575065 the gable end of a ruined barn is a useful landmark: aim slightly to the left of it and go on round the right shoulder of the next hill ahead.

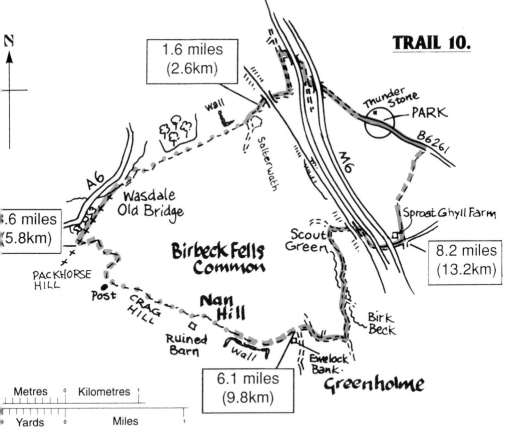

N

1.6 miles
(2.6km)

Thunder Stone

PARK

B6261

Wall

Salterwath

M6

Wasdale
Old Bridge

A6

Sproat Ghyll Farm

.6 miles
(5.8km)

Scout
Green

8.2 miles
(13.2km)

PACKHORSE
HILL

Birbeck Fells
Common

Post CRAG HILL

Nan
Hill

Birk
Beck

Ruined
Barn

Wall

Ewelock
Bank.

6.1 miles
(9.8km)

Greenholme

Metres 0 Kilometres

Yards 0 Miles

As you descend, the track gradually becomes clearer until you come to a wall on the right, which the track runs alongside, continuing to a T-junction where you turn left, swinging round immediately to the right down to the farm at Ewelock Bank (GR.589063) (6.1 miles: 9.8 km). At the farm turn left and follow the unfenced road half a mile (0.8 km) down to a T-junction where you turn left to go north to Scout Green a mile away.

This is a very narrow road running close beside the Birk Beck. There is very little traffic, but any which does appear may cause problems.

Just beyond Scout Green you turn sharp right and follow the unfenced road under the railway and under both carriageways of the M6, which here are

120 yards (110m) apart. After the second motorway bridge, ride on a few yards past Sproat Ghyll Farm and turn left through a gate (8.2 miles: 13 2 km), on to a hard track which is a bridleway. Ride up the track with the wall on your left, through a gap, and continue with the wall on your right. *This is the course of the Roman road from Low Borrow Bridge to Brougham, following the same route across Shap Fell as that taken by the railway and the motorway many centuries later.*

Bear right at an electricity pole, go on through a gate and along the edge of the next field with the wall on your right. This leads into a wide green lane and then out on to the B6261 at GR.607088. Turn left and ride half a mile (0.8 km) back to your starting place.

53

BRIDLEWAYS

HOW TO FIND YOURS

There are many miles of rights of way throughout the country on which you may ride: these fall into three types: they are Bridleways, Byways Open to All Traffic and Unclassified County Roads (which may be referred to as field roads or green lanes).

MAPS

The best maps to use while riding are the Ordnance Survey 1:25,000 (2.5" to the mile) Maps since these show the field boundaries. The maps of this scale, known as the Pathfinder Series, show Bridleways as a line of green dashes.

The Rights of Way information shown on a printed map was correct at the time that the map was printed but changes do take place: if you have any reason to query the Rights of Way information on a printed map it will be necessary for you to consult the Definitive Map and the County Council Rights of Way Officer to resolve the query.

The Definitive Map is a legal document held and maintained by the County Council; copies may also be found at County Council Area/Local/Divisional Offices and Parish Clerks' Offices and local libraries. The Definitive Maps are available for inspection by any member of public who wishes to see them. It would be a courtesy to telephone and ask for the relevant sheets to be made available.

**THE BRITISH
HORSE SOCIETY**

A 14 MILE (22 KM) CIRCULAR TRAIL (ANTI-CLOCKWISE)

A funeral party at
Swindale Head on the
old corpse road.

Ordnance Survey Map: The English Lakes NE Sheet (1:25,000)

Route: Toathmain - Swindale - Mosedale - Stackhouse Brow - Kemp Howe - Lanshaw Hill

Parking & Starting Point: A hard standing at GR.530165 on the unfenced road between Toathmain and Rawhead, one and a quarter miles (2.0 km) south of Bampton Grange.

Trail Grade: 2. Most of the way this ride is straightforward, but there may be some problems of boggy going in Mosedale. The route would not be accessible to 4WD vehicles between Dodd Bottom (GR.504116) and Thorney Bank (GR.555122). The North West Water Company's private road from Burnbanks to Kemp Howe may not be accessible until early 1995.

Route Description:

Ride southwards along the unfenced road towards Swindale. After half a mile (0.8 km) you come to a crossroads: keep straight on, with Swindale Beck on your left.

(As an alternative you could turn right and ride on the Water Company's road to Burnbanks, turn left on the minor road to Haweswater, and left again after 200 yards (180 km) on the bridleway past Naddle Farm. This leads across the Naddle Beck, over the hill and down a steep slope to rejoin the Swindale road by Bewbarrow Crag (GR.521142). It would add two miles (3.2 km) to your ride).

The road continues for two and a half miles (4.2 km) from the crossroads to Swindale Head (GR.504126), sometimes unfenced and sometimes between walls but always quiet, almost secretive, apparently cut off from the outside world.

When you reach the end of the road, the bridleway continues straight on, through the sheep pens at Swindale Head, down a stony path to a wooden bridge. *As you pass through the farmyard you will see a sign pointing to the right to the Old Corpse Road, which was used to bring corpses from Mardale to Shap for burial. There is a legend about a pony which broke loose when carrying a corpse on this journey and was not recovered for five days, so that the funeral had to be postponed. The Corpse Road was last used in 1729.*

Continue along a well-defined track across Dodd Bottom: ahead you will see crags on every side, and Forces Falls slightly to your left. *It might be a* good idea to check your girth here! The path is quite straightforward up the first rocky knoll, then you have a level stretch where the path crosses a stream. If you stick to the path, which is fairly clearly defined, it becomes quite boggy. The going is much better if you make a small diversion by turning right before the stream, up a steep grassy slope; then turn left and cross the stream higher up, aiming to pass between the two rocky outcrops ahead of you. It is good going if you keep on the grass and avoid the reedy places as far as possible, keeping to the right of the path. When you are nearly at the top you will see a rock balanced on the skyline: keep to the right of that and you will come to a broken-down wall. The path follows this wall for nearly a mile, through a wicket gate and across one or two boggy places where you have to pick your way with care.

When you come to the end of the broken wall you will see the bridge across the Mosedale Beck on your left. The bridleway continues along the hillside almost to the next fence, where it meets the bridleway from Longsleddale (Trail 5); and then returns down to the bridge, but the mountain bikers have made a short cut. Cross the bridge (GR.507100) (5.6 miles: 9.0 km) or ford the beck and bear right along the side of Little Mosedale Beck: then the track zigzags up to the gate at the top of the slope.

Through the gate follow fell buggy tracks up the hill until you come to another, older, track which bears right, round the hill. The track soon becomes well-defined and, although still wet in places, is quite easy to follow. Ride on through three gates - *with views of Wet Sleddale Reservoir over the wall on your right* - past White Crag (GR.539116)

(8.1 miles: 13.0 km). *This old sunken road along behind the wall was the route by which slate from Mosedale Quarry was carried to the main road at Shap; in places it has filled in and become boggy, but it is quite easy to pick the drier going.*

On the map the bridleway stops abruptly by Stack House (GR.546124) but the sunken road continues along

Take the next left turn, 300 yards (275 m) further on (10.2 miles: 16.4 km), and follow the North West Water Company's road for three and three-quarter miles (6.0 km). *This is a private road which NWW kindly allows riders to use. There is little traffic, but please take great care to give way to their operational traffic, and to cause no disturbance. It is an unfenced concrete*

the wall until both turn sharply right, across a stream and down to the unfenced road near Thorney Bank (GR.552122). Turn left along the road, through the gate by the cattle grid and left at the T-junction.

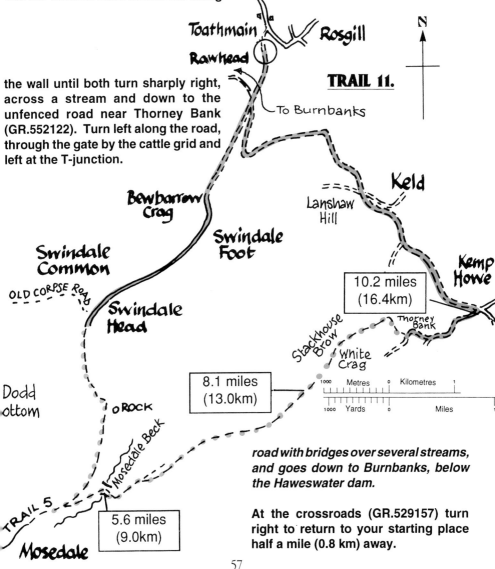

TRAIL 11.

road with bridges over several streams, and goes down to Burnbanks, below the Haweswater dam.

At the crossroads (GR.529157) turn right to return to your starting place half a mile (0.8 km) away.

57

CROSBY RAVENSWORTH TO ODDENDALE

A 10 MILE (16 KM) CIRCULAR TRAIL (ANTI-CLOCKWISE)

Ordnance Survey Map: Sheet 597 and The English Lakes NE Sheet.

Route: Crosby Ravensworth - Maulds Meaburn - Meaburn Hall - Morland Bank - Reagill - Threaplands - Oddendale - Lane Head.

Parking & Starting Point: Parking is available in a small lay-by at the north end of Crosby Ravensworth at GR.622154; otherwise limited kerbside parking in the village.

Trail Grade: 1. This is a pleasant ride on quiet country roads, and bridleways across enclosed farming land and on Crosby Ravensworth Fell.

Route Description:

Ride out northwards along the minor road towards Maulds Meaburn, *a very attractive village which you see at its best from this high level approach.* At Meaburn Hall, half a mile (800 m) further on, turn left, signed for Morland and Penrith. *Meaburn Hall is a fine Jacobean house, with two summer houses built later.*

Follow this road for one and a half miles (2.5 km), through the wood up Morland Bank, and turn left at GR.612187, signed for Reagill one mile further on. *There is likely to be very little traffic on these roads.*

Turn right at the T-junction in Reagill (3.6 miles: 5.8 km), and immediately right again on to another minor road. After 250 yards (220 m), opposite an old barn, turn left through a gate into a field (GR.603180).

Ride up the field, keeping a line of trees half-way up on your right, to a gate on the ridge; down across a stream and bear left towards a gate in the far left-hand corner of the next field which leads across another field to the back of Threaplands farm buildings.

Rather than go into the yard the farmer would prefer you to turn left and immediately join the gravel track which leads a mile southwards to join the minor road at GR.599164. Here turn right, and take the next turning to the left on to the minor road beside Wyegill Plantation which goes on to a T-junction half a mile (800 m) away (GR.598155).

At the junction, ride up the grassy track ahead which leads to Iron Hill. *Through the gate near the top there are cairns, a stone circle, and ancient disused quarries.*

Over to the right there looms the massive modern quarry at Hardendale which produces limestone for making steel. They blast three to five times a week and a warning siren is sounded one and a half minutes before blasting. There is no danger, but the blast may frighten horses, so take care.

The grassy track continues south-westwards through a gap between two intake walls to join the unfenced road (GR.592135) (7.2 miles: 11.6 km) which leads into Oddendale. Continue on a gravel track with the hamlet on your left and turn left on to grass at the end of the wall. Ride due east with the wall on your left, passing the deserted farmhouse of

Lane Head. *700 yards (640 m) further on the bridleway crosses the course of the Roman road, Wicker Street, which goes on northwards past the large ancient settlement of Ewe Close down in the valley. (Another bridleway from Oddendale back to Crosby Ravensworth, via Dalebanks,* is accessible but is not preferred because it has many gates.)

The bridleway bears left to go downhill north-eastwards into Town Head on a track called Slack Randy. *Here you are on the same route as Trail 13, but in the opposite direction.* Turn left (GR.621140) on to the minor road which leads northwards into Crosby Ravensworth. At the T-junction in the village turn right, and your starting place is half a mile up the road. *For a short distance here you are on the route of Trail 14.*

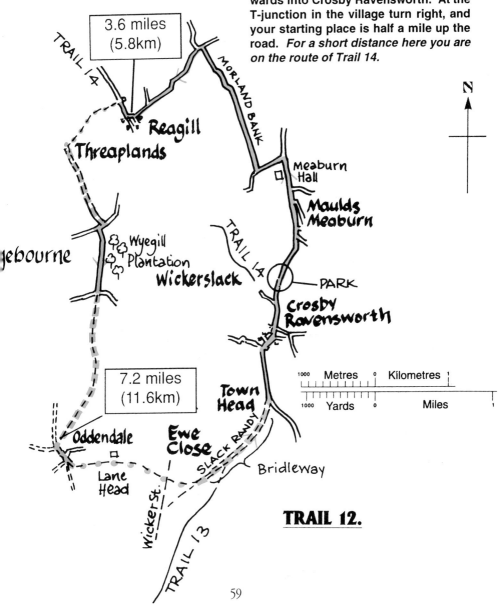

3.6 miles (5.8km)

7.2 miles (11.6km)

TRAIL 12.

59

BED AND BREAKFAST FOR RIDERS
ONE FAMILY ROOM AND ONE SINGLE ROOM
HORSES CAN GRAZE OR BE STABLED

FENTON AND CHRISTINE BRASS
BARNSKEW, MAULDS MEABURN
PENRITH, CUMBRIA CA10 3HU
TELEPHONE: (0931) 715218

MEABURN HILL FARM

Bed and Breakfast for Horses and Riders adjacent to Westmorland
Horse trails and bridleways. Relax after long days beside a log fire
and sleep in antique filled rooms (all bedrooms en-suite), with
views over village green and tranquil river valley.
Enjoy real farm breakfasts, afternoon tea, & simple suppers, with
grazing or stabling for your horse.
TELEPHONE MRS. RUTH TUER , MEABURN HILL FARM,
MAULDS MEABURN.(5 Miles west of Appleby) for more details.
0931 (Ravensworth) 715205

ORTON TO CROSBY RAVENSWORTH

TRAIL 13

A 13 MILE (21 KM) CIRCULAR TRAIL (ANTI-CLOCKWISE)

Ordnance Survey Maps: Sheets 597, 607 and The English Lakes NE (1:25,000)

Route: Orton - Knotts Lane - Gaythorne Plain - Crosby Ravensworth - Town Head - Sproat Ghyll

Parking & Starting Point: There is a car park in the centre of Orton village (GR.622083), and this is your starting point. It is also possible to park at Crosby Ravensworth (GR.621148) or by the B6261 (GR.600091).

Trail Grade: 2. This is a pleasant ride in limestone country. The going is quite easy but there are places where good map-reading is required, which are better avoided in mist.

Of Interest:

On Asby Winderwath Common there are hundreds of acres of limestone pavement with not a tree in sight. This is because sheep grazing prevents trees getting up. Before sheep farming expanded in the Middle Ages many of these pavements would have been covered with a light, broken canopy of ashwood, with Hawthorn and other shrubs, together with woodland herbs such as Dog's Mercury with still persists, along with rare ferns and other rarities, in the crevices between the blocks of stone.

The limestone pavement itself was formed millions of years ago in the Carboniferous Era. In the still water of shallow seas the calcareous shells of myriads of small animals fell to the sea bed to lie undisturbed, sometimes building up hundreds of feet depth of sediment which turned to limestone rock under the pressure of further deposits. Earth movements and changes in sea level eventually raised these rock beds to the surprising levels at which we now find them.

The characteristic fragmentation into blocks, known as 'clints', and crevices, known as 'grikes', is caused by variable solubility of the rock structure, taking place as slightly acid water filtered down through the overlying soil, much of which has now been eroded away. As we can see from the bridleway, the pavements and their edges or 'sears' are much disturbed by rock removal. Throughout history, stone has been quarried to construct local buildings and the miles of field walls. More recently larger-scale quarrying has permanently devastated large areas with consequent loss not only of features of geological importance but also of the habitat of many rare plants. Happily the conservation argument has now prevailed, and there is much closer planning control of limestone quarrying.

Route Description:

Ride out from Orton south-eastwards along the B6260, past the George Hotel. Bear left at the end of the village on to the B6261. At the crossroads (GR.629080) go straight ahead on to the unclassified road. Turn left up Knotts Lane, a bridleway, (GR.639079)

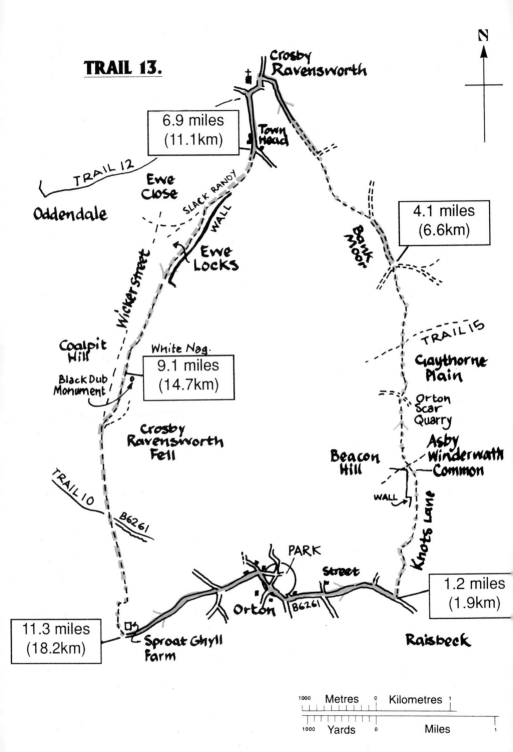

TRAIL 13.

N

6.9 miles
(11.1km)

Crosby
Ravensworth

Town
Head

TRAIL 12

Ewe
Close

Oddendale

SLACK RANDY

WALL

4.1 miles
(6.6km)

Bank
Moor

Ewe
Locks

Wicker Street

TRAIL 15

Coalpit
Hill

White Nag.

9.1 miles
(14.7km)

Claythorne
Plain

Black Dub
Monument

Orton
Scar
Quarry

Crosby
Ravensworth
Fell

Asby
Winderwath
Common

Beacon
Hill

TRAIL 10

WALL

B6261

Knots Lane

PARK

Street

1.2 miles
(1.9km)

11.3 miles
(18.2km)

Orton

B6261

Sproat Ghyll
Farm

Raisbeck

1000   Metres   0   Kilometres   1

1000   Yards   0   Miles   1

62

(1.2 miles: 1.9 km); go through a gate and continue northwards, keeping the intake wall on your left. *The grassy track passes a small reservoir and follows the contour at 1100 ft (340 m), with the High Pike of Great Asby to the right.* You leave the wall on a corner and the track becomes vague: careful navigation is required between the limestone outcrops - *beware hidden rabbit holes* - to a high wall marching across the fell from east to west. The gate which you want (GR.640100) is at right angles to the track, not over to the right where the wall bears north-east. *The views here are magnificent and described at the start of this trail.*

Beyond the wall there are several vague tracks: keep going due north, leaving Beacon Hill with its old shallow quarry on the left, and ride between the pavement outcrops to the track leading to Orton Scar Quarry, on the right, which is still in production. Continue north down the hill to Gaythorne Plain. The track becomes vague again, but aim for the right-hand of two round clumps of sycamore trees. *Trail 15 crosses your route at GR.641113.* You meet the B6260, unfenced here, at the junction at GR.639124 (4.1 miles: 6.6 km).

Follow the road for a few hundred yards, now joining with Trail 14, and bear left on the byway at Bank Moor, opposite the old quarry (GR.637130). The byway goes across the open fell to a minor road at Bank Head leading down into Crosby Ravensworth, where you turn left and ride through the village.

On the right stands the parish church, dedicated to St. Lawrence. It was originally built in the 12th century and has been altered in a succession of styles since then. Behind the church stands Crosby Hall, the manor house probably

built in the 15th Century on the site of an earlier building. It is now a farmhouse. Just off the road to the right there is a ford where you can water the horses. Ride south to Town Head (GR.621140) (6.9 miles: 11.1 km) and fork right on to a bridleway called Slack Randy going south, then south-west and rising. At the fork (GR.615132) bear left and ride along the bridleway, a gravel track, with the wall on your left. *On the right you come to the ancient settlement of Ewe Locks, one of many in this district; it has never been excavated but appears to have consisted of two stone houses and associated buildings.*

Half a mile further on, the wall turns away and the bridleway continues south-south-west between the limestone outcrops of Wicker Street and White Hag to pass the monument at Black Dub (9.1 miles: 14.7 km). *This marks the place where King Charles II rested with his army on the way south from Scotland on 8th August 1651. Nearby is the site of a shooting box where Lord Lonsdale, the 'Yellow Earl' entertained his guests in such a luxurious style that it has become part of the local folklore. This was formerly a heather moor where grouse were common, but bracken has taken over in recent years.*

Ride on to join the line of the Roman road known as Wicker Street which leads down across the B6261, and follow the grassy track up the hill with the wall on your left - beware rabbit burrows. After half a mile (0.8 km) you bear right, leaving Wicker Street; cross the line of the gas pipe by two access gates, and aim towards the corner of the wall (GR.602079). Follow the wall down to Sproat Ghyll Farm (11.3 miles: 18.2 km). Turn left on to the road, which has little traffic, and go on to join the B6261 to Orton, one and a half miles (2.4 km) from Sproat Ghyll.

BANK MOOR
TO MORLAND

TRAIL
14

A 19 MILE (31 KM) CIRCULAR TRAIL (CLOCKWISE)

Ordnance Survey Maps: Sheets 597 & 598 and The English Lakes NE (1:25,000)

Route: Bank Moor - Crosby Ravensworth - Reagill - Sleagill - Newby - Morland - Kemplee - King's Meaburn - Burwain Hall - Jerusalem - Seat Hill - Drybeck - Maskriggs Wood.

Parking & Starting Point: Parking is available at the start of your ride, on the turf at Bank Moor, (GR.637129).

Trail Grade: 1. A pleasant ride through mainly pastoral country.

Route Description:

Leave the road on the byway which runs north-westwards from opposite the old quarry (GR.637130). Your route follows the turf-covered track across open fell for three-quarters of a mile (1.2 km), when you meet the farm road at Bank Head. Follow this road into Crosby Ravensworth (1.6 miles: 2.5 km). Turn right on the road towards Maulds Meaburn.

St Lawrence's Church, immediately on your left, is a church of great architectural interest. Dating originally form the end of the 12th Century, it has been modified and partly re-built over the years and now displays a succession of styles from Early English to Victorian Gothic.

After a quarter of a mile (0.4 km) (GR.622153), turn left on the bridleway signed for Reagill. Go through the metal gate to the right of the farm track; do not follow the track itself. Ride up the field towards Croke Trees and out on to the track through a gate which, like all the gates on this bridleway, is a specially installed equestrian gate. Follow the track for a few yards, then turn right and immediately left through a gate into the field.

For the next mile (1.6 km) you follow an attractive route, clearly waymarked, across a succession of fields towards Reagill Grange. *On the right, (GR.615163), there is a good example of a traditional Cumbrian bank barn. Taking advantage of the sloping ground, there are entrances at two levels. The lower level was traditionally used to house stock over the winter, and their feed was stored above.* Further on, go through the gate (GR.610165) on to the track, and follow it to Reagill Grange (3.3 miles: 5.3 km). *This is a fine old farmhouse with cylindrical chimney stacks, another traditional Cumbrian feature which is now seldom seen. The house was originally medieval and has been extended several times, most recently when the northern wing was built in 1700.*

After passing the house, bear right on the road towards Reagill. *At GR.606174 there are fine views of the Pennine range to the right.* In Reagill, (GR.604178), bear left at the Y-junction; at the T-junction turn right, following the road to Sleagill. When you reach the village, a mile further on, turn left and immediately right, as signed for Newby, one and a quarter miles (2.0 km) away. *These are narrow roads with few verges, but there is fortunately little traffic.*

At GR.591207 turn right on to a byway (signed for Newby), an attractive green lane between hedges. Bear left at the next Y-junction, (GR.592208). You join the road opposite Newby Post Office (6.4 miles: 10.3 km); turn right here and follow the road towards Morland.

This one mile (1.6 km) length of road is also narrow with no verges; care must be taken, although there is little traffic. In Morland take the first turning right, signed for Bolton. At the Crown Inn turn right towards Maulds Meaburn. Follow the road with the beck on your left, past the King's Arms. Next to the white footbridge, cross the ford, which has a hard surface. Bear left on to the road, and continue up the hill to join the major road. *Look out for traffic from the left.*

At GR.604224, near the top of the hill, turn right on a bridleway, signed for Bolton, which passes Highgate Farm. *Here you can visit the Animal Trail to see little Dexter cows, sheep, donkeys and lots more; there is a place to leave your horse while you have a cup of tea.* The bridleway goes on to Kemplee and down to the River Lyvennet. *The footbridge is the only way across the river, and although passable for horses, it is rather narrow and you would be wise to dismount and lead.* Continue on the track through the wood, and turn right at GR.618221 on to the minor road towards King's Meaburn.

This was once a drove road, as betrayed by its wide verges. As you enter King's Meaburn, note the open areas between the older sandstone houses. Local people provided stances or 'service stations' with lodging for the drovers, and folds for their cattle between the houses. At the far end of the village, turn left (GR.622209) (9.5 miles: 15.3 km) on to a bridleway signed for Chitty Hill. *This is a hard track with verges, between hedges;* it turns sharp right and then left, continuing uphill past Sockenber Farm. *The track becomes overgrown as it leads into a small wood.* At the end of the wood, (GR.637213), turn right and ride towards Burwain Hall, keeping the fence on your left. At GR.639210 ride on through the next wood, leaving the track which swings right. Go past Burwain Hall and on to the minor road (GR.644198) (11.9 miles: 19.1 km). Go straight along this road, which has a wide grass verge.

After one mile (1.6 km) turn right on the track to Jerusalem Farm. At the farm go straight on along a lonning between hedges. At GR.654186, where a gate to the left is marked Private, bear right. Continue up the hill with the hedge on your left. Go through the gate into the next field, continue with the hedge on your left, and then aim towards a gate in the stone wall opposite about 200 yards (180 m) from its left-hand end. Ride up the hill with the wall on your right to join another bridleway on a well-defined field track. Turn right along this track, joining the road at Seat Hill, (GR.648179) (14.6 miles: 23.5 km), about half a mile (0.8 km) further on.

Turn left on this minor road, then after a mile (1.6 km) turn right on to the B6260. After 350 yards (320 m) turn left on a minor road signed for Drybeck. A mile (1.6 km) further on, as you reach the village of Drybeck, turn right along a straight track which becomes a bridleway after a mile, and leads into Maskriggs Wood (18.2 miles: 29.3 km). *A quarter of a mile (0.4 km), to the left there is a fine view of Gaythorne Hall, a Jacobean house with an interesting plan, the porches and*

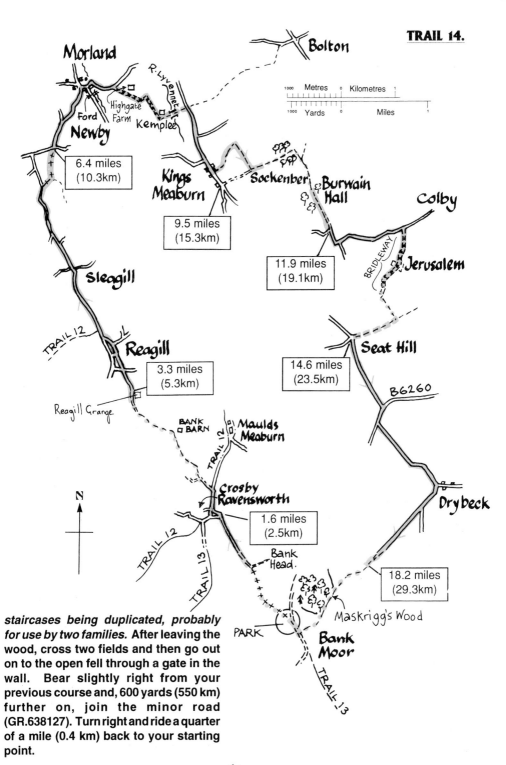

Morland

Bolton

Highgate Farm

Ford

Newby

R. Lyvennet

Kemplee

1000 Metres 0 Kilometres 1

1000 Yards 0 Miles 1

6.4 miles
(10.3km)

Kings Meaburn

Sockenber

Burwain Hall

Colby

9.5 miles
(15.3km)

11.9 miles
(19.1km)

BRIDLEWAY

Jerusalem

Sleagill

TRAIL 12

Reagill

3.3 miles
(5.3km)

Seat Hill

14.6 miles
(23.5km)

B6260

Reagill Grange

BANK BARN

TRAIL 12

Maulds Meaburn

N

Crosby Ravensworth

Drybeck

1.6 miles
(2.5km)

TRAIL 12

TRAIL 13

Bank Head.

18.2 miles
(29.3km)

Maskrigg's Wood

PARK

Bank Moor

TRAIL 13

staircases being duplicated, probably for use by two families. **After leaving the wood, cross two fields and then go out on to the open fell through a gate in the wall. Bear slightly right from your previous course and, 600 yards (550 km) further on, join the minor road (GR.638127). Turn right and ride a quarter of a mile (0.4 km) back to your starting point.**

67

ORTON TO TARN MOOR

TRAIL 15

A 10 MILE (16 KM) CIRCULAR TRAIL (ANTI-CLOCKWISE)

Ordnance Survey Maps: Sheets 607 & 597 (1:25,000)

Route: Orton - Raisbeck - Sunbiggin - Tarn Moor - Maisongill - Hollin Stump - Gaythorne Plain - Broadfell

Parking & Starting Point: Parking is available at your starting point in the centre of Orton village (GR.622083).

Trail Grade: 2. Careful, accurate riding is needed among the limestone pavements. The rocky area between Tarn Moor and Sunbiggin is not accessible to vehicles.

Of Interest:

The land round Orton is good grazing land for sheep and cattle, with drystone walls separating the fields. The road to Raisbeck has wide verges, indicating an old drove road. Sheep and cattle were driven from Scotland and Northern England on these traditional routes to markets further south. When permission was given to enclose land adjacent to these drove roads, it was stipulated that sufficient width must be left for the large flocks and herds to pass. The resulting verges now provide ungrazed refuges for many plants and their associated fauna which could not survive in the grazed and mown fields alongside.

The stone walls beyond Sunbiggin (GR.663086) are a good example of traditional drystone walling. The two faces of the wall are built up separately, the stones being placed 'end-in, end-out' and each one crossing the joint between the two in the course below. The middle of the wall is packed with rubble as it rises, and at intervals a course of 'throughs', long stones laid right across the wall, bind the two sides. In this wall two courses of 'throughs' can be seen as lines of projections from the wall face. At the top the wall is finished with a course of 'cams', regular stones laid on their edges. Walling styles vary tremendously and even within Cumbria some people claim to be able to tell where they are by the walling!

Tarn Moor is of great importance for nature conservation and is easily damaged. Heather grows in acid, peaty conditions which are found near the surface but the underlying limestone can be seen exposed in places and obviously there is seepage of lime-rich water draining off the limestone hills to the north. Thus, shallow-rooted plants favouring acid conditions grow alongside deeper-rooted ones penetrating to the limy stratum below. Where ground water reaches the surface in depressions, there are rich tracts of marsh with orchids and many other uncommon plants.

On the left at GR.628098, there is a well-preserved example of an old limekiln built into the hillside in the traditional way. A cylindrical chamber, open at the top, narrows to a throat at the bottom, which in turn opens into an arched recess at the front of the building. Firing material, normally wood, was fed in conveniently from ground level at the top, alternating with layers of broken limestone. The whole was then lit through the throat, and when combustion had completed the breakdown of limestone to quicklime, the lime and ash

69

were raked out through the arch. The lime so produced was, of course, used for spreading on fields to correct acidity and for making mortar for building.

Route Description:

Ride out from Orton south-eastwards along the B6260, past the George Hotel. The road bears left at the end of the village. Half a mile (0.8 km) further on the B road turns right at a cross-roads (GR.629080), but you should carry straight on.

After a mile and half (2.4 km) you reach Raisbeck. Turn left (GR.645075), signed Sunbiggin. *This is a very narrow road between stone walls. There is little traffic, but care is needed.* At Sunbiggin (2.9 miles: 4.6 km), one a half miles further on, bear right and go to the end of the metalled road, where it leads on

to an attractive bridleway, wide between stone walls (GR.663086).

The bridleway leads through a gate on to Tarn Moor, where the vegetation changes dramatically, with dense heather dissected by meandering green tracks and marshy areas. Keep strictly to the bridleway because Tarn Moor is of great importance for nature conservation and is easily damaged.

You soon reach a bridleway crossroads where you go straight across; then turn left at the next one (GR.672083) and ride up the hill to a gate in the wall. Going through the gate, follow the wall on your left, not the track which bears half-right. Keep near the wall for three-quarters of a mile (1.2 km) until it returns to the left; then ride north-westwards on a track between the limestone pavements which is marked by posts.

70

TRAIL 15.

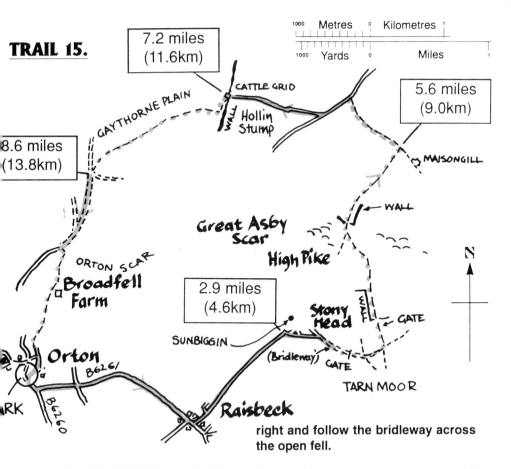

7.2 miles (11.6km)

5.6 miles (9.0km)

8.6 miles (13.8km)

2.9 miles (4.6km)

1000 Metres 0 Kilometres
1000 Yards 0 Miles

CATTLE GRID

GAYTHORNE PLAIN

Hollin Stump

WALL

MAISONGILL

Great Asby Scar

High Pike

WALL

ORTON SCAR

Broadfell Farm

Stony Head

GATE

SUNBIGGIN

(Bridleway) GATE

Orton

B6261

TARN MOOR

RK

Raisbeck

B6260

N

right and follow the bridleway across the open fell.

Bear right (GR.667099) on to the bridleway from Sunbiggin to Great Asby and follow it down the hill to a gate in the wall near the corner (GR.668102). Go through the gate and ride north-eastwards with the wall on your right (not on the left as the OS map shows). Continue through three fields until you come to a bridleway on the farm road (5.6 miles: 9.0 km), and then turn left. Ride down to the minor road (GR.668117) and turn left.

Follow this minor road for one and a quarter miles (2.0 km) up the hill to the cattle grid (GR.652118) (7.2 miles: 11.6 km). Immediately turn left, on to good turf, and keep the wall on your left. After 200 yards (180 m), turn half-

The track is not easy to see, but careful map-reading between the limestone pavements will bring you out on to the B6260 road (GR.632108) (8.6 miles: 13.8km). Turn left.

On the left is the road to Orton Scar Quarry; it produces fine limestone which can be polished almost like marble, and is used for high quality flooring. Immediately after the next cattle grid (GR.628098), take the bridleway down a narrow track to the left which leads out into a field. The bridleway continues past Broadfell Farm to arrive in Orton village. Turn right at the road, right again, and then left to arrive back at your starting point in the centre of the village.

71

RAVENSTONEDALE MOOR TO CROSBY GARRETT AND SUNBIGGIN

TRAIL 16

A 16 MILE (25 KM) CIRCULAR TRAIL (ANTI-CLOCKWISE)

Ordnance Survey Map: Sheets 596 & 597 (1:25,000)

Route: Ravenstonedale Moor - Crosby Garrett - Whygill Head - Asby Grange - Maisongill - Sunbiggin - Tarn Moor - Middle Busk

Parking & Starting Point: Parking is available beside the unenclosed road one mile (1.6 km) north-west of Newbiggin-on-Lune (GR.693063), close to your starting point.

Trail Grade: 2. Careful, accurate riding is needed among the limestone pavements. The rocky area between Maisongill and Sunbiggin would not be accessible to emergency vehicles.

Of Interest:

In contrast to the heather-clad moor round Sunbiggin Tarn, Crosby Garrett Fell is almost entirely grassy. At least in part, this must be due to heavy grazing, which heather cannot stand. Indeed, heather moor is now a nationally threatened vegetation type for this reason. Under heavy grazing heather is replaced by more resilient grasses and sedges. Here, the dominant plant through which the bridleway passes is the tussocky and rather unpalatable White Bent Grass.

Where limestone rock lies close to the surface the coarse White Bent Grass gives way to close-cropped fescues, and there may be molehills. This shows that White Bent favours the more acid, glacial drift soil, and where this thins out the limestone influence allows growth of lime-loving grasses which are 'sweeter' and therefore

more closely grazed. The molehills show that this limy soil is fertile enough to support earthworms, the favourite food of moles.

From Ladle Lane (GR.726098) you can see several 'field houses' in nearby fields. Each 'field house' consists of a hay barn and a cow byre. The crop from the field is gathered into the barn and in winter cattle are housed there to eat the hay on the spot. Manure goes back on to the surrounding fields. Thus transport of hay and manure between field and farmstead is avoided, and it is only the farmer who has to walk up to do the work. It is a traditional dales farming system, unfortunately now in decline though highly efficient in energy conservation.

Out on the high ground near the top of Newclose Lane, (GR.713091) looking east, you have a magnificent view across the fertile Eden valley, thick with hedgerow trees, to the whole sweep of the Northern Pennines including Cross Fell, the highest point (2930 ft, 894 m) on the Pennine range. In contrast, if you look west and north of the Howgill Fells, you will see the Lake District mountains with their more jagged peaks formed of highly resistant volcanic rocks.

Near Whygill Head (at GR.702109) the ground is very wet. One narrow field on the left is under water, at least in winter, and birds attracted to it include Mallard and Redshank. In the drier fields further on hares may be seen, easily distinguished from rabbits by their larger size, much longer legs giving them greater speed, and carrying their tails down when running away so that the white 'scut' is not seen.

Approaching Asby Grange, a few large, roundish boulders lie in the fields. One, close to the bridleway, can be seen to consist of a coarsely granular, pinkish rock. They are granite 'erratics', that is rocks carried from elsewhere, in this case from the Shap area, on glaciers and left marooned when the glacier finally melted 10,000 years ago. Continual grinding and rolling during their icy journey has produced the rounded shape and smooth surface. Just beyond Asby Grange on the right there are two small relict woods with old Ash trees growing out of crevices between blocks of limestone. This shows that trees can grow in such conditions, and Ash is the species best adapted to them.

At Sunbiggin Tarn (GR.674086), the marginal reeds give way on the landward side to rich growths of Mealy Primroses and the like. These primroses, and Hoary Plantains with their flat, hairy rosettes of leaves and pinkish flower spikes also grow on the road verge. Except in winter, the whole area round Sunbiggin Tarn is dominated by Black-Headed Gulls which nest here. This creates a conservation problem, as the gulls' droppings so enrich the ground that the orchids, Mealy Primroses and the like are replaced by docks and nettles! Many other birds, including Coot and several species of duck, are also to be seen in the Tarn area.

As you descend towards Ravenstonedale, splendid views allow you to compare the long horizontal summits of the Carboniferous Era Pennine Fells to the east with the rounded outlines of the geologically older Ordovician and Silurian Howgill Fells to the west. They differ in appearance because the younger Pennine fells are capped with hard Millstone Grit rocks which have resisted weathering. The Carboniferous strata were laid down more recently (geologically speaking) than the Ordovician and Silurian strata, and should therefore outcrop at higher altitudes. However the Dent Fault, a long crack in the rock sheet, has allowed the Carboniferous

Pennine rocks to the east to drop to the level of the older Howgill rocks, so that rocks separated by millions of years in age now lie side by side.

Route Description:

Turn on to the bridleway which runs north-eastwards along the wall on the fell side for three-quarters of a mile (1.2km), to a junction (GR.702067). Here there is a choice of three tracks. Take the left-hand one, which in fact is a byway.

For the next one and a half miles the route is not easily seen on the ground, and careful map-reading is necessary. **Follow the byway north-eastwards towards Crosby Garrett one and a half miles (2.4 km) away. Ride under the viaduct carrying the Carlisle to Settle railway line -** *if you are lucky you may see a steam train* **- and turn left in the village (GR.728094) (3.1 miles: 5.0 km).** *Crosby Garrett Church is a fine medieval church in a splendid situation high on a hill at the north end of the village.*

Leaving Crosby Garrett, the ride passes briefly through hedge country. Shortly after crossing the bridge over the Carlisle to Settle railway there is an example of how woodland can spread if grazing is prevented: the wide banks between the track and the boundary hedges themselves are colonised by sapling Ash trees and Hazel, Hawthorn and Rose scrub.

From the village join a bridleway on a track called Ladle Lane, which crosses the railway on a narrow bridge (GR.726098). The track turns left after three-quarters of a mile (GR.717095) on to a very narrow track between high stone walls. The way back on to the fell is through an attractive old wrought iron gate, and by bearing right at GR.712088

you join a bridleway which goes northwards towards Newclose Lane. Newclose Lane, one and a quarter miles (2.0 km) long, is an unmetalled road leading on to a minor road; here turn left (GR.718110). *At Water Houses on the left of the road there is a picturesque footbridge, both uprights and footway being composed of dressed limestone slabs.*

After one mile you will come to the crossroads at Whygill Head (GR.704108) (7.2 miles: 11.6 km). Ride straight across, on the road towards Great Asby, and turn left on to a bridleway, through a field gate 100 yards past the crossroads.

The next one and a quarter miles (2.0km) to Asby Grange requires careful map-reading, and the first part is boggy. Go through the gate at the end of the narrow field, bear left (GR.701110) with the wall on your left, and turn left at the end to go through a small wicket gate. At the wall junction, go through the gap and bear right, with the wall on your right (GR.697108). As the wall veers away to the right keep going straight on across the field, through two gates, and then through a third gate out on to a farm road (GR.689107).

On the corner at Asby Grange leave this road and turn left (GR.684106), where the bridleway follows a track across the field. The track continues through several field gates to Maisongill, where you join the farm road. 300 yards (275 m) past the farm, turn left (9.4 miles: 15.1km) on to a bridleway signed Sunbiggin Tarn and Sunbiggin. Ride up the hill through three fields, with the wall on your left (not as shown on the OS map). Through the gate (GR.668102) the bridleway goes between limestone pavements - keep

TRAIL 16.

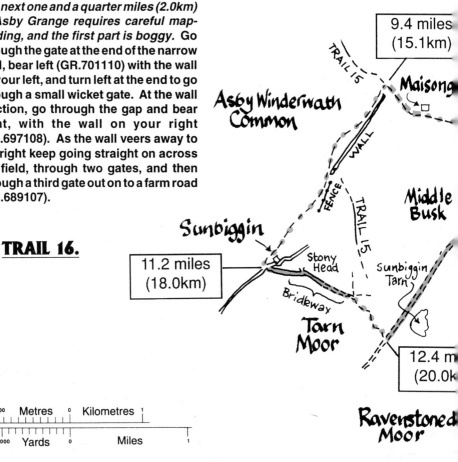

9.4 miles (15.1km)

Maisong

Asby Winderwath Common

Middle Busk

Sunbiggin

11.2 miles (18.0km)

Stony Head

Sunbiggin Tarn

Bridleway

Tarn Moor

12.4 m (20.0k

Raverstoned Moor

Metres Kilometres
Yards Miles

the fence on your right until you go through a waymarked gate (GR.667098), then continue south-westwards with the fence on your left. A post on the skyline shows the route, which is through a very narrow defile between the pavements. Go through the narrow gate near the corner of the wall (GR.663093) and follow the bridleway across four fields towards Sunbiggin Farm. The bridleway leads into a narrow green lane between stone walls which comes out on to the road at Sunbiggin (11.2 miles: 18.0 km), where you turn left.

The road ends at Stony Head and leads on to a wide bridleway between stone walls. You ride through a gate (GR.667083) out on to the open moor, and very soon there is a bridleway crossroads where you turn right (GR.669082), and a little further on bear right again. One and a quarter miles (2.0 km) from Sunbiggin you reach the minor road past Sunbiggin Tarn, (GR.674086) (12.4 miles: 20.0 km).

Turn left on to the road, which is an unfenced minor road with little traffic. Ride on the road, not on the verge, for the few hundred yards from the bridleway to the cattle grid, to avoid damaging plants.

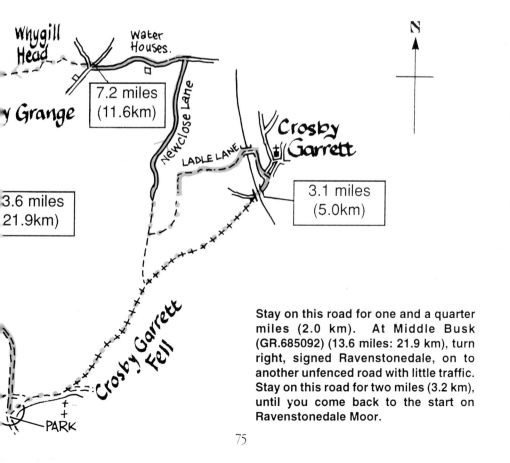

Stay on this road for one and a quarter miles (2.0 km). At Middle Busk (GR.685092) (13.6 miles: 21.9 km), turn right, signed Ravenstonedale, on to another unfenced road with little traffic. Stay on this road for two miles (3.2 km), until you come back to the start on Ravenstonedale Moor.

THE BRITISH HORSE SOCIETY

The British Horse Society was founded in 1947 when two separate equestrian bodies - The National Horse Association and the Institute of the Horse and Pony Club - decided to join forces and work together for the good of both horse and rider.

It is a marriage that has proved to be a great success and the British Horse Society has steadily increased its membership from just 4000 in the late 1960's to over 60,000 in the 1990's.

By becoming members of the British Horse Society, horse lovers know they are joining a body of people with a shared interest in the horse. Members can be sure that they are contributing to the work of an equine charity with a primary aim to improve the standards of care for horses and ponies. Welfare is not only about the rescuing of horses in distress (which we do); it is also about acting to prevent abuse in the first place. There are many means to achieving this: by teaching and advising, by looking to the horse's well-being and safety, by providing off-road riding, by encouraging high standards in all equestrian establishments, and fighting for the horse's case with government and in Europe.

The British Horse Society works tirelessly towards these aims thanks to the work of its officials at Stoneleigh and its army of dedicated volunteers out in the field.

Membership benefits the horse lover as well as the horse; the Society can offer something to all equestrians, whether they are weekend riders, interested spectators or keen competitors. The benefits include free Third Party Public Liability and Personal Accident insurance, free legal advice, free publications, reductions to British Horse Society events, special facilities at the major shows, and free advice and information on any equine query.

Largely financed by its membership subscriptions, the Society welcomes the support of all horse lovers. If you are thinking of joining the Society and would like to find out more about our work, please contact the Membership Department at the following address:

The British Horse Society
British Equestrian Centre
Stoneleigh Park
Kenilworth
Warwickshire
CV8 2LR
(Telephone: 0203 696697)
Registered Charity No. 210504